The Individual Team:
How Fairness Wrecked the Workplace.

Blaine Little

For information on bringing the author to your organization,
call (615) 513-6443 or visit www.MomentumSeminars.com

Dedicated to my wife Hannah

and our daughters,

Elisabeth and Amanda.

These beautiful ladies remind us of

the importance of family.

We love having you as part of the team.

Table of Contents

PREFACE 6

SECTION 1 – THE TEAM 9

HOW A TEAM COMES TOGETHER 9
THE DIFFERENCES THAT DEFINE US 21
POLITICAL CORRECTNESS AND OTHER BAD IDEAS 39

SECTION 2 – THE TEAM MEMBER 53

TO TEAM OR NOT TO TEAM 53
MEMBERSHIP HAS ITS BENEFITS 65
OBLIGATIONS EACH MEMBER OWES THE TEAM 73
THE INDISPENSABLE TEAM MEMBER 89
GENERATIONAL DIFFERENCES 97

SECTION 3 – THE TEAM LEADER 111

A LABOR OF LOVE 111
DIVERSITY AND ITS FALLACY 119
MORALE – GOOD OR BAD, IT FALLS ON YOU! 149
DUPLICATING YOURSELF 167
MAINTAINING THE STANDARD 187

ABOUT THE AUTHOR 207

Preface

Though, it may be for the viability of the company or even the good of the community, bringing people together is a necessary part of progress. However, it is no easy feat. There may be aversion or outright resistance to goals or new ideas. Aligning everyone to move in the same direction takes a small miracle.

I have traveled the country training and speaking to professionals about sales, leadership, better communication and building teams. My company, Momentum Seminars Training & Coaching brings me to all sorts of work environments. People have confided in me what they dare not share with management or even best friends.

From being a follower to a leader or simply studying other teams, there is a lot to unpack in terms of what makes an organization successful. I have had the good fortune to be a fly on the wall and see the inner workings of several companies. In this book, I relate observations, experiences and patterns I have seen in working with some of these organizations.

There is an attempt by some individuals in North America to apply a "*one* size fits all" posture to subordinates or even coworkers. This generality is not practical nor is it sustainable. That mentality brought into the workplace by idealogues, or even those meaning well is also one of the determinants for so much turnover in the workplace.

Unfortunately, there are a lot of well-intentioned and perhaps generally accepted practices that pull teams down rather than build them up. In business today, there are as many cultures as there are organizations. So, a universal approach to team building is difficult, perhaps impossible. But patterns of team building can be a great help for identifying where you stand at any given time.

Nothing throughout the following pages is off the table. Many of the current norms are discussed, some in depth. But if you are a business owner, it is still up to you to decide what policies to implement that will shape the morale and even your corporate culture. If you are an employee, it is up to you to decide whether to work there or not.

In this book, I discuss the importance of establishing a relationship with each person in your workplace. But relationships, even professional ones, take time. That means understanding what motivates or demoralizes others in the organization. It is an investment in time, energy and emotion. But it is an investment that pays off.

The book you are holding is divided into three sections. The first will discuss the team in general. What it is and what it is not. We look at how the group is almost a living thing in and of itself. And as with all living things, it will change over time. Nothing is predictable, but there are always clues that can be spotted when one is looking for them.

Section two is for the individual team member. This is the biggest portion of a company, and all parts must be moving in the same direction for success. One of the biggest challenges, especially in today's workplace, is dealing with generational differences.

In the third section, we take a look at what it takes to be an effective team leader. The majority of supervisors in America received no managerial training whatsoever. Many times an employee who was proficient at the prior job got the promotion. But being a good technician does not necessarily make one a good leader.

Lastly, I will say a heart-felt **thank you** for the purchase of this book to add to your development library. My hope is you will gain new insights into how teams come together and move toward success, whether that success be organizational, personal or toward the improvement of others.

How a Team Comes Together

What do you get when you take half a dozen stray cats, put them all in a burlap bag and give it a good shake? The answer is: you get six really pissed-off cats! Yet, this is what happens time and time again in American businesses. They will throw a random team into an office bullpen and wait to *"see what happens."* This is not a good strategy.

So, what makes a group want to function as a team? If there is a startup company or simply a new or expanded department within an organization, what is the secret sauce that makes its' individuals <u>want</u> to work together? And what if the culture is a new one or not yet formed?

A team will eventually take on a life in and of itself. After all, a business corporation is a group legally recognized as an entity itself. That being the case, all groups move through their own cycle of life. And that growth is for the most part predictable. It would be a benefit for all to understand how that lifecycle will develop and what it might look like in the future.

Much in the same way, professional athletes come together as teams, businesses and their people will also coalesce. They show up for training camp where the industry veterans can knock off the rust from the seasonal break while the rookies stick out like sore thumbs. There is a sort of blueprint in that. Everyone knows who the coaches are and that they're watching. It's about getting in shape and having the right mindset, but it's also a time for developing relationships, both good and bad.

Individual players are sizing up one another to assess who they think will make it and who will get cut. In football, ninety athletes show up on the first day of training, but that number is cut by almost half before the regular season. With that level of pressure, there will undoubtedly be clashes of personalities and the occasional dustup.

Often, the coaches or even the team captain will have to step in from time to time to keep the peace. But once everyone knows where they fit in, a mutual respect develops. Even an athlete who has a personality clash with someone else will put away pettiness to move the team forward. Hopefully, the final roster will be good enough to make it to the playoffs.

For many, there is a notion people will simply come together because, after all, everyone is a professional, right? No, not right! Long before people were employed or considered an expert at what they do, they were human. As such, human beings are filled with prejudices, insecurities, bad attitudes and personality flaws that should not get in the way of their work. And yet it happens.

Dealing with the issues of others is often messy. It can leave others scratching their heads asking *" What did I do?"* when they didn't actually do anything wrong at all. There is often social fallout from an individual trying to figure out where he or she fits.

When entrepreneurs talk about the tribulations or bumpy patches of the early days, they are speaking as much about poor communication and personality clashes as they are about product failure or funding issues. Synergy doesn't happen overnight. And there will inevitably be rough patches before there is smooth sailing. But this is all part of the process of forming a team.

In the mid-twentieth century, the U.S. Military was aware of cohesion and group dynamics but did not understand exactly how teams were formed. In fact, the term "team" was not widely used at that point outside of athletics. Today, it's referred to in the United States Army as *unit integrity*.

It's the ability for individuals to come together in a culture that moves everyone toward a common goal. An army simply cannot fight an enemy with each soldier going his own way. They must be united in their mission as all effective teams are.

In 1965, the U.S. Navy desired to better understand the specifics of how groups grow, but there were no books or in-depth research available. There was a thought that if the growth of a unit was understood, it could be observed and therefore predictable. That knowledge would be important to diagnose why one group becomes dysfunctional when another excels.

Bruce Tuckman, a behavioral scientist for the Navy discovered and codified what that lifecycle looks like. Though, at the time, he had little information to go on other than some magazine articles and the occasional scholarly paper. But as he poured over what printed material he could, Tuckman noticed a pattern emerge. Teams grow through four initial levels;
1) Forming,
2) Storming,
3) Norming and
4) Performing.

Eventually, the scientist would add to this model a possible fifth and final stage. But the overall concept is one many branches of the Armed Forces still teach in its leadership courses today. Here is a breakdown of each phase...

Forming
This first stage is the orientation of a group. Just like Spring training in baseball, people are sizing up one another as well as trying to identify who each would prefer to work with closely. Generally, people dress to impress and are on their best behavior. No one wants to be the first to upset the apple cart. That would put a bullseye on their back or be grounds for dismissal altogether.

Though this is the *honeymoon period,* individuals may still test the boundaries of one another, though in subtle ways. The intent is to see who is a push-over, and who will fight back. Toes may be stepped on, for which the offender will quickly and profusely apologize. Especially if it were no accident. Everyone is scrambling to claim their territory. And everyone wants as big of one as possible, whatever that territory may look like.

And by *territory*, I mean authority, clout, control and power. This could be the corner office, an assigned geographic sales area with the highest median income, or even an arbitrary title. Have you ever seen two people fight over the word "assistant"? There is a strong fear (and it is fear) that one may be stripped of responsibilities one day or out of a job completely. Without people, places and things saying we are important, we begin to doubt it ourselves. It's about staking your claim, in a nice way of course.

Management is most influential at this point and tries to assure everyone has the tools and skills necessary to do their jobs. Encouragement from on high goes a long way here and is necessary to set the tone of what will eventually become the culture. Otherwise, cohorts will not believe there to be any managerial support.

At this early and tenuous time, there needs to be a certain amount of hand-holding and oversight. The absence of veteran members or a power vacuum altogether will most likely lead to paranoia. Of course, this attitude would kill what should be a thriving workplace before it gets off the ground. This brings us to the next section.

Storming
At this stage, the honeymoon is over. Apologies occur a lot slower in this timeframe, if at all. And those who had their boundaries previously tested might now push back in not-

so-delicate ways. Conflict is inevitable and cliques will start to form. Leadership must address the issues by correcting unacceptable behavior and coaching employees in a spirit of progress.

It can seem like everyone is out for themselves, and in fact, that may be the case! The psyche of many individuals shifts from *"What do I want"* to *"What can I salvage"* as the fear of missing out goes into high gear. With subtlety out the window, some will drop the façade altogether.

At its worst, it can be a political game of king of the hill. Some will be like chickens with their heads cut off running around to see where they fit in and whether someone else is trying to take their spot if they haven't already. No doubt, management will be brought in to settle petty squabbles that have little or nothing to do with the job. In a word; drama!

Some will be fine with tension and others will be almost visibly shaken or seem to just give up, put off by the game. The reason for the upset is that there are no clear-cut responsibilities, boundaries or culture. Not yet anyway. It is at this point, a company may lose good, talented people who simply do not wish to play office politics.

A good supervisor will be certain to reassure the team these are simply growing pains, though the drama is not to be tolerated. Management will be tested. A boss should be ready to guide anyone back toward their own responsibilities.

As I will discuss in the leadership section, I am not in favor of pitting team members against one another. However, this is an opportunity to observe the strengths and weaknesses of each individual. It is critically important management use this time to size up members of the team. These are all good assessments to take and remember for more legitimate threats to the organization in the future.

Some of those competitive skills may come in handy one day. Who exhibits grace under pressure? Who comes up with good ideas despite the pressure? Who can be trusted or not? Who loses their cool and is the potential office hothead? Yes, it may be necessary to make cuts before the regular season of play.

A team **does NOT** want to be stuck in the storming phase! And yet, some companies are in this dysfunctional holding pattern for years. Some tell-tale signs are poor quality control, bad customer service, lawsuits, HR complaints and a lack of training. After a while negativity becomes part of the accepted culture. Top-tier leadership is to blame for allowing this type of atmosphere to grow and normalize.

Negativity breeds negativity. The best potential staff members in town may never seek employment with the company because it has such a bad reputation. This creates a vicious cycle of low morale and high turnover. The right leadership can turn things around, but it also takes money, attention, the right people and time.

However, if the initial conflict is more about how to best move the team forward, this can sometimes be a sign of growth, which is what every team should want. Yes, conflict can be good if it is for the right reasons and its energy is steered in a positive direction. This will be a function of management. Again, take notes as to how people behave during this time.

Norming

Here, individual responsibilities are accepted. People know the strengths and weaknesses of one another and are aware of when others may need help. Each person's responsibilities are much clearer, even if it's not spelled out in a policy manual. Things aren't perfect in this phase, but they are starting to fall into place.

Roles are understood and relationships develop. Even those staff members who don't see eye to eye with one another are beginning to get over it and accept their positions. Hopefully, roles will be filled by the right people but if not, it will be just a matter of time before everyone notices. If positions are out of place, a manager needs to reshuffle the team to find the best fit possible. Many times those who know they do not fit in will leave if not already asked to do so.

There is a sense of security in knowing what to expect from day to day when an organization is normalizing. In the development of children, we see the importance of consistency. That is also important to the productivity of personnel. Fretting over whether the boss is in a bad mood from day to day or whether there will be layoffs soon deprives an adult of attention to the work at hand. But routine creates an atmosphere of certainty.

Opinions are expressed without the fear of ridicule. This is significant because trust is developing among the team and its management. This spirit of openness allows for collaboration and should be fostered. Trust is an important ingredient for any well-functioning operation.

Performing

In the performing phase, the group truly functions as a team and is where you as a team member or manager want to be. Morale is good. Employees are more self-regulating and tend to resolve conflicts themselves. Everyone knows the goal and sees the vision of where the company is going. Management can more easily delegate tasks with less involvement themselves.

This is true proficiency. An organization is almost on autopilot. Without people wondering where they fit in and all the drama, individuals simply get to work. Job satisfaction is high and so is output. This means less employee turnover and more productivity which leads to greater profit for the corporation.

When we think of a successful company, school or church, this is the model we want! However, a unit can still regress to an earlier, inferior level of synergy and proficiency. This could be a sign of poor management and something I wrote about extensively in my book for new managers.

In the case of brand-new leadership or broad-sweeping policy changes, an institution could be pushed back into the Norming Phase. Everyone notices how some of the roles may have shifted. While a company's rocky financial footing or even rumors of layoffs would place it into Storming.

A few years later in his studies of team formation, Bruce Tuckman added a possible fifth segment. This was in light of the fact not all groups are enduring. Should the organization or project come to an end, it enters into a fifth stage, what I call...

Transforming

This is the end of the lifecycle for an ad hoc committee, task force or project management team. Everyone moves on to their next assignment. Though, it could also be the end of an enterprise completely. Some call this the "mourning" phase because the party is over.

Hopefully, leadership will take the opportunity to recognize the efforts of others and achievements will be celebrated. This transition may also occur due to a company acquisition or merger. In this case, the process starts all over again for the individuals.

Having addressed the different phases of organizational development, it is important to heed a few warnings. The first two apply to timeframes. There is no set time as to when the group will move to the next period of growth. One cannot say, *"By June, we will finally have moved out of the Storming Stage."* It is wishful to think it would be that straightforward.

After all, we are dealing with the least predictable force on the planet; people. There are no guarantees in this arena. But with good management, and a clear direction to follow, a team can make transitions fairly effortlessly.

Communication is key as to who does what, and perhaps most important, **why**. The direction and purpose must be repeated like a mantra. Otherwise, team members will second guess what they and their colleagues are to do.

This creates a difference in priorities and lack of security which is so closely related to Storming.

It's really about the growth of the team. Individualism is great, so long as the employee's talents are being channeled in one direction. Where one personality makes demands, others will resist. This creates stagnation and an inability to progress.

This brings us to the next warning. A team does not want to fall into a rut. Being stuck in a particular stage, other than Performing, is detrimental to the growth of an organization. Storming is perhaps the worst part of the growth in which to be caught.

And yet, many corporations find themselves there for years. Many good employees will abandon a corporation that does not get its act together in a reasonable amount of time. People want to feel like part of a winning team and expect to see growth.

Prominence trumps growth in the Performing Stage, however. If a company is already well established and has a good reputation, the good employees of competitors may seek out greener pastures. Success breeds success. Why else would so many college students wish to attend Yale, Harvard, or any other Ivy League school?

For those coming into an existing organization, team formation will be minor because it is already formed. New hires need to perceive what the culture is and understand the group will NOT bend to them. The new guy will have to learn to adapt despite his level of expertise. Unless of course, that new guy is the boss, which is a completely different scenario.

19

Aside from the occasional fly in the ointment who seeks undue attention, people appreciate a certain amount of consistency as to what their job is and the environment within which they work. The Performance Stage delivers that. Constant change and ambiguity will create turmoil and division. Though routine can lead to stability, the search for uniformity can be problematic, however.

The Differences that Define Us

Everyone responds differently to the chief motivators of pain or pleasure. Also, everyone will have different perspectives and therefore different priorities for the same event or situation. To uncover the motivations and priorities of another, a manager must first have an individual relationship with all members of the team. Of course, every supervisor does have a relationship with each member of the team but if he or she is not cognizant of what that relationship is, it is more than likely a bad one.

Of course, relationships among teammates are important as well. A team is a collection of individuals. Unique people have the notion to move in different directions without the guidance to make them move as one. This is their nature; people go where they think they should be.

A six-person team moving in half a dozen different directions doesn't move the ball down the field. It's not acting as a team at all. The group has to understand where it is going and why. And that direction cannot be antithetical to where the individuals want to go themselves.

In 2021, Netflix was at odds with many of its workers over a comedy show that was said to be insensitive to some individuals. There was a walkout of employees in October of that same year. Several months later, the streaming service amended its statement on the Netflix culture;

"Not everyone will like—or agree with—everything on our service... we program for a diversity of audiences and tastes; and we let viewers decide what's appropriate for them, versus having Netflix censor specific artists or voices.

As employees, we support the principle that Netflix offers a diversity of stories, even if we find some titles counter to our own personal values. Depending on your role, you may need to work on titles you perceive to be harmful. If you'd find it hard to support our content breadth, Netflix may not be the best place for you."

There is a lot of truth to that. Not every workplace is for everyone. It's not the job of corporate America to create an alternate universe for each one of its employees. Netflix even went so far as to include a *"Disagree, Then Consent"* provision in the same memo. It takes into account a difference of values among its thousands of employees, though the work is still to be completed.

No one is necessarily right or wrong for having different points of view. However, if values are starkly different from organization to the individual worker, there will undoubtedly be friction. Values, both personal and corporate, are important as they should serve as a roadmap for how to achieve overall goals. It is always good to ask, "Is this a good fit? Is this where I need to be?" The right fit is vital in the workplace.

During the COVID pandemic, the majority of office workers began doing their jobs from home. After two years, however, many managers felt subordinates were so disengaged and the quality of collaboration had suffered. Leaders felt it was time for teams to return to the office.

But that's easier said than done and many resisted the re-entrance. Both Tim Cook of Apple and Elon Musk of Tesla issued edicts as to when their people were to go back to the facility. As with several companies, the mandate was compulsory and failure to do so would lead to termination.

Employees knew of the requirement to show up to work the day they were initially hired. Coding, graphic design and sales calls while still in pajamas had become the new norm. But convenience does not change the corporate culture. There are still thousands of places to work remotely, but Apple and Tesla are not two of them. Undoubtedly, many of those employees have sought out a place that will be a better fit for them.

For years, I have wondered why anyone would want to work in a department, company, or industry where they are miserable. Yet, millions will retire this year having done exactly that for their entire careers. I feel it is important one find joy in what he or she does. This also applies to the type of work being done as well. We will discuss that more in-depth in a later chapter.

But people do want to feel as though they belong. Each should find his or her work fulfilling, or they could be a hindrance to the overall operation of the group. For instance, Gallup* has conducted research that shows job satisfaction is generally more important than salary to most workers. So there needs to be a fit for the employer and its employees.

This is a shift in perspective from considering the collective to understanding each component of the whole. This is what I call: *The Individual Team.* But for many, there is a belief everyone should be of the one mindset with the same outlooks and priorities. This runs counter to how humans progress and yet we see this fallacy being told, taught, and trained in the workplace.

Let's take a trip to an office park not such a long time ago and not so far away, to see how two different people perform at the same job. Abbey was hired as an administrative aid. Frank, a regional manager, hired her as a replacement for an assistant who recently retired but had been with Frank for over a decade.

Abbey's tasks are in part, social media marketing, planning, scheduling and the filing of several reports, order forms, and even legal documents that still must be stored as hard copies. She is replacing Phyllis, a long-time employee of the company. Phyllis was said to be meticulous and *"on top of it"* when it came to getting her manager where he needed to be. In the past, Frank had to do little in way of supervision with his assistant, things simply got done and his office ran efficiently.

Abbey does well with most planning as she can coordinate upcoming projects with other members of the department. Working as part of a team is enjoyable for her. She also enjoys the marketing aspects of the job. Though it is online, she still feels a sense of connection with others, even at a distance.

However, after a few days, Frank notices several file folders piling up on the corner of Abbey's desk. He almost knocks over the stack going into his own office. When it's mentioned Phyllis would never let things go this long, Abbey promptly puts the paperwork away, but the boss has to say something about it every other day.

A few months into her tenure, it is noted there are several scheduling conflicts and travel isn't ordered until just a few days before Frank is to leave town. Furthermore, the hotels are several miles from the stores which Frank is to visit. As he must travel a fair amount, the boss explains the importance of booking flights early. Not just from a cost-saving benefit, but to get flights earlier in the day and choice seating as well.

As one may guess, Abbey is still playing Jenga with the file folders. Phyllis would never let it get this bad. She is asked to now finish all filing before she leaves for work each day. Abbey says she will comply.

Finally, one Wednesday morning Frank comes into the office, eyes bloodshot from the late flight the night before, and calls his assistant into his office. This time, she knocks over the paper obelisk herself. Frank knows something has to change.

Abbey is well-liked by the department and is close friends with several of the other administrative aids. When asked why she does well with certain facets of the job and all but neglects the other tasks, she tells her boss she is just not able to get into the right frame of mind with paperwork. Frank is baffled. She further states travel, and other scheduling issues just don't appear on her radar until a few days before.

Clearly, Abbey is a people person. But is she the right person for this job? After listening to Abbey about her preferences and even an attempt to give certain responsibilities to other assistants, the regional manager comes to a realization; Abbey IS NOT Phyllis.

But no two people are ever the same. Though, he remembers when the former assistant was new to the job. She was in many ways the opposite and loathed some of the marketing responsibilities. Frank finally understands where the young assistant's head is and sees the need for her to understand his point of view.

Any attempt to treat everyone the same is simply delusional. No two people are exactly alike. In addition to the carrot and the stick, there are several other dimensions of a personality we will discuss in a later section. But how we perceive motivation is many times affected by our experiences. If you have two or more children, you may not be surprised to notice how different each will react to the same set of circumstances.

If people are raised the same, share time together, live in the same environment, go to the same school, attend church with one another and are taught the same morals, by all logic their personalities should be identical. And yet, siblings have unique points of view. They will communicate in varied ways and create different priorities. Now before we go too far down the nature versus nurture path, I will tell you it's a bit of both.

Many times, it's not a matter of intellectual understanding at all. Shared events do lead to similar experiences, but those life lessons are colored by perspective. What the individual looks for is what they will see.

An attempt to change someone's perspective is an attempt to change a personality. Any of us who have been in a romantic relationship and tried to change our partner knows how that generally turns out. It is better to clearly express our own understanding and go from there.

Returning to the story of Frank the Regional Manager and his new assistant, Abbey, we see how a correction could be made. By stopping to compare his assistant to everyone else, especially Phyllis, he better understands Abbey and what motivates her. The boss comes to terms with reality and stops pining for his former employee.

Frank assesses Abbey to be a people person but not proactive or quite as task-oriented as he would like. Nonetheless, she shows up to work on time and has a positive attitude. She also does very well with all the other aspects of the job. The situation is what it is, and Frank accepts that. But it is also time for his employee to understand the reality of the job and what is required.

The manager holds out one hand as if it were one half of a weight scale and states: *"If these tasks can't be done, I will need to hire another person to perform them."* Abbey's eyes light up and her face beams from a new smile. But the boss continues looking at his opposite hand as it lowers. *"If*

I hire someone else, then I will not have that much for YOU to do here."

Abbey's smile immediately fades as she realizes he is talking about replacing her. For whatever reason, this has just never crossed her mind since she got along so well with everyone including Frank. It is simply a natural consequence that if work is not being done or to the level expected, one will find themselves out of a job. Theoretically, that should be true of any organization.

What may seem on the surface as a veiled threat to fire Abbey is nothing of the sort. Frank never said the word *"fired"*, raised his voice or even gave her a dirty look. It's not even an ultimatum. There is no malice at all. Rather, the conversation was a reminder of what the job is and why she was hired in the first place.

It's nothing personal. She may do well at another department or even in a different company, but if the work is not correct, there is simply no need to have her come to work for Frank. Abbey understands the seriousness of the situation.

She does her own assessment and decides she likes her company and the boss despite not being able to pick and choose her assignments. She has several friends, a close commute and doesn't want to leave. So, she put a plan together, one that more closely resembles the boss's priorities. On her business calendar, she creates a reminder to schedule quarterly travel three weeks out to get cheaper airfare and better flights.

She still begrudges paperwork but commits to completing it before each coffee break. That way, she has something to look forward to once it's complete and is sure to file at least twice a day. After a while, her new systems become more routine and less of a chore. The assistant takes pride in her work and feels a sense of accomplishment as a vital member of the team.

Every time Abbey receives a scheduling alert or sees a stack of paper, she is reminded her job is on the line because **this** is what her job is. As opposed to someone who might have created these systems in the first place, she is motivated by avoiding the pain of leaving a job she likes. It was not until she realized she would lose her comfort that she took action to be progressive about her career.

Sadly, most of us will not react until we see catastrophe looming on the horizon. We want the most we can have with the least amount of effort. Is that laziness, or just being human?

Though the new assistant should be commended for the turnaround, it was Frank who realized the difference in the personalities of the two assistants. Where a laissez-faire, or *hands-off* approach to management worked for Phyllis due to her being more proactive, it was necessary to be more attentive to Abbey.

In either case, Frank got the results he wanted, though there were two different approaches. A lack of understanding of what motivates Abbey would, over time, lead to misunderstandings, hurt feelings or division. But process and methodology are far removed from one's core values or personal needs.

Psychotherapist Cloe Madanes discovered half a dozen needs that are basic to all individuals. Unlike Maslow's classic Hierarchy of Needs, these attributes do not follow a prescribed order. Their importance is arranged by the individual and may even shift throughout stages of life.

The Six Basic Human Needs are chief motivators as to how people react toward any given circumstance. They are key to an individual as she establishes her priorities. This explains why two people can look at the same task or situation and view them with a different sense of urgency.

Security
This is a sense of comfort or certainty. What is familiar and routine in our lives plays a part in our happiness. It's a survival mechanism to want to know what to expect. The more important security is as a motivator, the less likely someone will be a risk taker.

Babies not only need feelings of love, but they need to be held to have an assurance of safety. Children who grow up without a sense of security tend to develop trust issues and become selfish later in life. Adulthood doesn't cause us to outgrow this need. It's always there to some degree.

Years ago, my wife and I attended a course to certify us as foster parents for the State of Tennessee. In one of the classes, we learned of the importance routine plays in the development of a child. Until that time, I had never really considered its importance.

But for many of the children that would come into the foster care system, they had no routine at all. No one told them when to sleep or wake up. No one was there to tell them to do their homework and when to stop playing video games. A lot of these kids had no idea where their next meal was coming from. So, providing a routine, gave them a sense of security they never had before.

Significance

The sense of importance can come to us in many ways. We may consider the number of friends we have, our title or how much money we make. It can also be the effect we have on others.

Significance or a sense of admiration from others is typically strong with most males. Remember the last time you went to a cocktail party or other reception? The cliché question upon men meeting one another is "What do you do?" This is our lead because we tend to have a strong sense of identity when it comes to our careers.

In the 1980's the Yugo automobile was introduced to the U.S. market. They were imported from the Soviet Bloc because they were fuel efficient and cheap. The Yugo was a decent little hatchback grocery-getter. After a couple of years, the imported car was met with much criticism.

Some say there were design flaws, but it was modeled after an Italian Fiat and the first couple of years of sales were fairly good. But the workers in the Yugoslavia plant simply stopped caring. Many of the workers would clock in drunk and there was little in the way of quality control. Craftsmanship went out the window and that was the end of the automotive company.

Yes, the "male ego" is a thing. And it's not entirely a bad thing, either. A sense of pride in our work is what made America so great. But whether male or female, we all need to feel as though we matter.

Connection

The word "Love" may be a little too familiar for the workplace. But there are so many types of love, it really shouldn't be. Ant member of a team needs to know they are respected and appreciated. Anyway, love is really what we're talking about there.

Everyone needs to be loved, they need to give it as well. Though it may not be at the top of everyone's list of importance. Connection assures us we are not alone. It's scary to think someone will not be there to help us when we are down or that we won't be there for them.

The perpetuation of love is a stabilizer in our lives. It helps us to grow emotionally, psychologically, and spiritually. Just as children never outgrow the need for a certain amount of security once they reach adulthood, the same is true for our relationships. Unlike the other five needs, love is the only one manifest as an emotion. Even introverts need to have a sense of connection with others.

Those without enough love or connection tend to be jealous of others and may even lash out. They find it hard to control their emotions. We can look at our prisons and find them filled with those who never had a strong parental figure or role model. Many without a father figure will join gangs to create a sense of family.

Growth

Here, we are talking about growth on a personal level. It may take the form of a promotion at work or earning a degree, though it need not be quantifiable. It could also be as simple as the self-esteem we feel by accomplishing a task.

When I was in high school, I asked a substitute teacher what degree she was working on. She said it was in history. So, I naturally asked if she was going to become a teacher since I didn't know what else one would do with that degree.

She stated, *"Many times, an employer just wants to know you can complete something. It means you will more likely be a reliable employee".* Perhaps she was right.

There are a lot of people who work in industries not related to their degree, whether by design or not. And not all reliable employees come to us the way we anticipate. What makes a good team member is a willingness to adapt and gain new skills.

But personal achievement is not a high priority for everyone. The adage "If you're not growing, you're dying" seems a little harsh. People can celebrate accomplishments in different ways, even if that growth is not easily visible. The main thing is we realize our growth and keep pursuing our potential.

Also, those who expect proof of certification should be aware, life doesn't always hand those out. This can lead to a discrepancy in priorities from one person to the next.

Always encourage the personal progress of others no matter what it looks like or how long it takes.

Interestingly, researchers have long held an individual cannot increase one's IQ or intelligence. And yet, it appears people can grow their "EQ" or emotional intelligence. There is now even what is considered social intelligence. It's all about making YOU the best possible.

Variety

Variety is the "spice of life". A break from routine is what makes life interesting. And if every day seems to be the same, we say we are in a rut. We feel trapped and this can take a heavy toll on relationships.

Generally, we all like surprises when they are the good kind. Even an unpleasant random situation can provide a challenge and help us to grow. Too much variety, however, can make us appear restless and not provide stability in our lives.

I once heard a story of a young man who owned a lawn care service. He ran the company for years, ever since he was a teenager. His enterprise put him through college, and he even had a few employees. It was a success, but he got tired of laboring in the hot sun and decided to sell it.

Instead, he decided to pursue a more "mature" career, something in personal finance. He passed all the necessary state exams and found a firm that would show him the ropes and get him started. He picked an office cubicle and off he went.

But it all went South pretty quickly. Being inside, in the same temperature-controlled environment each day, doing the same work, was too much to handle. It's not he didn't have a work ethic; he had already proven that. But the similitude of one day to the next made his skin crawl. He only lasted a few weeks before he went back to lawn care.

Contribution

Why do **we** feel good when we help others? It may be a sense of mercy or just that we are the best suited to fill a need. But for some, helping others is a calling.

Those who are at the top of their game will tell you they learn so much by helping others. When something good happens to us, we want to share that experience with others. In part, because we want confirmation, but also to show others can have good fortune as well.

Any serious martial artist will tell you; they BEGIN to learn once they become black belts and instruct others. This is true of most instructors no matter the field. It's because of all those principles that were instilled in us, we now see from a different perspective.

I have often wondered what is meant by the term "the heart of a teacher". Does it take a certain personality to instruct others? Well, it certainly takes patience.

We have all had bad teachers. From elementary school to college, there have seen those to which I wondered "What the hell is this person doing here"? Not everyone has the temperament to teach. Perhaps it is the case of those who cannot make use of their degrees.

35

Of course, imparting knowledge is not the only way in which people assist others. Consider all the doctors, nurses, first responders and therapists who do their part to make the world a better place. We may not think of those in sales as helping others, but indeed, they promote products and services which help others to grow.

As stated earlier, not everyone will assign the same priority to these Six Needs. And this is where there could be an impasse about how to proceed with a task. Our principles are often created by our needs.

A few years ago, my wife and I were planning a little getaway. Just a long weekend with the kids a short drive away. Nothing too fancy, but someplace new.

We all wanted somewhere restful and with good restaurants. Museums or other educational sites for the kids were a plus. We couldn't decide where to go, so I suggested a novel approach. I went up to the attic and grabbed something out of a board game. It was one of those compass spinners you flick with your finger when it's your turn to play.

I placed it on a paper map laid out on the table. Wherever the game piece stopped, we would drive a few hours in that direction. It would be a fun little adventure.

Before I could even get my finger into the flicking position, my wife, a Librarian, said the idea was dead on arrival. There was no way she was going to leave three or four days completely up to chance. I even suggested throwing a dart at the map. Again, it was a no-go.

Here is where security and the need for variety came to odds. For me, an enjoyable vacation would be seeing where we landed and what the universe had in store for us. But that would be stressful for at least one member of the family.

This happens all too often in business and life. The goal or destination is the same, but how to get there is at odds. So, I left the planning of our trip completely to my wife.

Much to my wife's credit, she heard me out and understood my fear of having a boring vacation. She listened and understood what was important to me. As it turns out, it was one of the best trips we ever had.

Conduct an assessment yourself and see how you might differ from others. Rank each need in YOUR priority, 1 through 6. There is NO wrong answer.

_____ Comfort	_____ Significance	_____ Growth
_____ Variety	_____ Connection	_____ Contribution

Priorities are many times difficult to reconcile. But if we consider the other person's perspective, we can at least understand one another. A lack of understanding is many times what keeps a team from coming together.

A difference in priorities can easily create conflict, which is why good communication is so important. We will now take a look at what else may create division within a team.

Political Correctness and Other Bad Ideas

"The notion of political correctness has ignited controversy across the land. And although the movement arises from the laudable desire to sweep away the debris of racism and sexism and hatred, it replaces old prejudices with new ones."
-President George H.W. Bush, 1991

There are public ideals that move in and out of phase from time to time in our society. That of political correctness has been lingering for a few decades. If you thought this concept had played itself out, you are unfortunately wrong. Just as someone in business or the military calls it for the nonsense it is, someone from academia or politics puts a new spin on it. Otherwise, how would those devoid of original thought ever have any influence?

As stated previously, no two people are the same. Though a sense of uniformity would be convenient for those in power, it is a lofty goal. In fact, it is an impossible one. Still, organizations try.

After all, armies around the world make soldiers the same from head to toe. But this is just window dressing. The way one looks says nothing about his morals, work ethic or level of initiative.

Perhaps one of the best ways to achieve the goal of sameness is by attempting to guide the process and actions into one, unique perspective. This may be accepted to a degree if it is part of the corporate philosophy, and everyone is on board with it. But when an attempt is made to alter who an individual is, expect push-back.

I have had the good fortune to travel to China on several occasions. Though it was business related, visiting that beautiful country was truly a blessing for me. I was happy to experience all the history, culture, philosophy, and art. Upon my first visit, it was the people who surprised me the most.

If I may be allowed to generalize; the Chinese were sweet, gentle and very intrigued by Westerners. Even in Beijing, Hong Kong and other large cities, the people were nice and hospitable, which is uncharacteristic for many metropolitan areas throughout the world. These people were thankful for visitors and if they understood English, were quick to start up a conversation with me.

When I wasn't tending to business, I enjoyed museums, visited bazaars and tried new restaurants. I typically had a translator with me, but if not a kind stranger, usually a college student with a good knowledge of English would be nice enough to answer my questions and show me the sights. I made good use of their hospitality and took in as much as I could, too.

How sad it is that these bright, sweet, hardworking people live under a regime of limited human rights. Officially, they have no human rights unless they are Party members. But the Communists in China are far too smart to publish a list of what entitlements their citizens do NOT have. It's a life of ignorance by omission.

If there is ever an infraction, such as free speech, police will not beat down someone's door and take them away in handcuffs. That would be too disruptive. Generally, they will send a single messenger or perhaps even just a letter for the individual to report to the police station at a prescribed time. Given citizens are not allowed to leave the country, their province or even their home village, they have no choice but to report. THEN they are made aware of what rights they do not have.

Case in point, I had spent a week on the mainland and had a one-day layover in Hong Kong for the return trip. At that time, Hong Kong due to its economic power had a free media. In my hotel room, I saw a news segment from the very Province I just left. It reported how people were arrested for protesting there.

The only thing I saw on mainland TV were Communist award ceremonies and children's choirs singing patriotic songs. No reports of arrests, or anything negative for that matter, were televised. Almost as though there were never any civil disturbances.

But there were. Apparently, some factory workers felt the work conditions were not safe in their shop. They weren't necessarily mad; they just wanted the issues resolved so they could work in a healthy environment. It's at the very least a fair request. Something we take for granted in the West.

But when they were not able to secure a solution or get the attention of the appropriate government bureaucrat, they took to the perimeter of the factory to get noticed. They hoped to capture the attention of upper management or the public in general so others will know what the issues were inside the facility. Well sorry comrade, you can't do that!

"One country, two systems" was a Chinese national slogan that was touted and even revered by the government and many of its people as a noble system of unification. I find it to be reminiscent of the *"separate but equal"* credo during our own civil rights movement in the U.S. In both cases, they have nothing to do with equality or even equity.

But that report played out on my hotel room television set, and I was struck by the dichotomy of the country. Some citizens had certain entitlements and others had none. By the way, the one foreign news outlet that was allowed to broadcast in Hong Kong was CNN. You can make out of that fact what you want.

Now just imagine living in a place where an individual may not be allowed to express an original thought. Because of that, what might otherwise truly be a good idea will never see fruition. Or imagine that saying something contrary to the norm might threaten your livelihood.

Your life has a black cloud hanging over it. The paranoia sets in so deep that you are afraid to say things to your children for fear your ideas will be repeated in public. The entire day is one long game of "gotcha" as others in the community lie in wait for you to slip up so you will be publicly humiliated, or worse.

Also, imagine after a while, the threat of humiliation becomes instant shame within yourself simply for having a thought contrary to societal norms. After all, if that thought were spoken aloud, it could bring instant condemnation. You allow the habit of self-editing to become part of your makeup as an individual, your personality. All because an institution or public perspective deems what is right and what is wrong for you.

You don't have to go to a Communist land to experience this type of personality molding, it's an everyday reality in American business. Instead of government, it comes to us from the media, idealistic training or individuals who never had an original thought in the first place.

There is plenty of bad advice out there making its way through company corridors and being championed as corporate gospel. This false doctrine has no shortage of its disciples either. They hold themselves up as experts and try to change the zeitgeist of the day.

It is the ad executive who avoids the term "light" in a beer commercial to not offend people who may be fat, dark or blind. It's the lawyer who offers an opinion less on legal merit but on a philosophical vendetta with the other side, thereby killing the deal. It's the company that would continue to pollute the local area because it bought enough carbon credits or would plant trees elsewhere.

Political correctness compels organizations to make bad decisions when they should otherwise focus on motivating their people toward productivity or the achievement of a goal. And yet, few leaders are shouting, "Enough of this!"

Being PC isn't about eliminating rudeness and making the other person comfortable, that's called manners. Instead, it is a way of controlling the thoughts, feelings, speech and actions of others. It's peer pressure for adults. But its targets resent the notion and an organization that tolerates it.

When you can't wish someone *"Merry Christmas"* because you might offend a non-Christian, though the majority of the country at least identifies with Christianity, priorities are out of order. I don't know of anyone who has ever been forced to repeat the salutation. Though, I can only imagine some insist they were somehow slighted or perhaps even their civil rights were violated. But there are simply a lot of overly sensitive people. This goes to a lack of personal maturity.

Also, it shows a lack of confidence in one's ideas. If one is resolute in a belief, that person should not be offended that others hold different beliefs. The insistence on an idea standing alone without contrary points of view, without scrutiny, only shows it to be a weak idea in the first place.

In December, when one of my Jewish friends says *"Happy Hanukkah"* to me, I might state a more generic Holiday hello, but more often than naught, I return the greeting in kind. After all, my recognition of Hanukkah does not delegitimize Christmas. And I do want my friend to be happy during his celebration.

You cannot protect the rights of the minority by completely ignoring the wishes and expectations of the majority. Though, that exact argument is prominent in our society today. It's a fallacy that if society is not bending to every social demand, Democracy will fail. That's the opposite of Democracy, it's chaos.

But there is a lot of money to be made and power to be gained by chaotic politicians and their pundits, at either end of the political spectrum. By never letting a good crisis go to waste, the pot keeps getting stirred. The public remains in motion to move toward... whatever. Did you think all those hats and bumper stickers were free?

If you want to see real civil rights violations, go to China, North Korea or Viet Nam. These governments are not given to every whim or new idea. This is why Communist countries are so opposed to religion. There is no distinction between philosophy, psychiatry, history, religion or politics. There is only one way to think, that of the state or its dictator.

But in a free society, people may believe whatever they wish and who is anyone else to judge? When those who subscribe to a particular thought attempt to coerce others into that point of view, a line is crossed. Social pressure to use certain words or adopt activities that are counter to our own principles is an attempt to alter character. In short, it is brainwashing.

But I have noticed those without moral principles in the first place are the ones most given to this seduction of thought. Any belief system or code of conduct looks good to those without a set of values.

And this is who would-be autocrats prey on. They are useful idiots who do not know or care when they are committing actions that violate the rights of others. They are formless but can be turned into irrational ideologues.

This all too often plays out in corporate America under the guise of sensitivity training or the latest "critical" thinking. Today, most seminars of this sort are less about individuals working together and more about assigning people to a faction, based on gender, color, age or almost a dozen categories. This is contrary to the concept of a team. Instead of bringing unity, it creates division.

Political correctness is nothing more than culturally sanctioned aggression. It's less about inclusiveness and more about shaming or assigning labels to dissenters. And that creates discord and thus stifles collaboration. Those who are lacking any personal fortitude wrap themselves in this false sense of justice, not because they believe in it, but because it is the only power they have. It's their playbook and they are the modern-day grade school hall monitors.

Hypersensitive instructors have done more harm than good when it comes to professional development. Before I launched my career as a corporate trainer I would many times sit through workshops myself, some elective and some required for the entire department. Many corporate seminars were thoughtful and engaging.

But on occasion, I would hear some information I thought to be suspect. So I did what any rational adult would do, I looked up the law, guidelines or policy for myself. People can do that with the Internet, you know. And fact-check they will!

Attempting to scare the hell out of someone so they will do right, has never been a good teaching device. People are always going to check your information and call BS when it's discovered to be manufactured. If one point is proven to be false, people tend to dismiss the entire message.

That message may be a good one overall, but one sticking point could ruin the credibility of the information. It is better to deal with plain truth and perhaps most important, explain WHY a law, regulation or company rule is in place. Not everyone's actions are motivated by emotion and fear is a poor threshold for morality.

What we as members of an organization should be seeking is understanding. Though, not necessarily compliant with that which is superficial. Refraining from certain words or terms does not change anything in the physical world. Calling a manhole a *"maintenance tube"* does not change the fact there is a hole in the middle of the street.

I was once in a meeting where another facilitator used the term *"rule of thumb."* As a figure of speech. A woman spoke up and stated she was offended by hearing the idiom. The leader at the front of the room was puzzled and asked why she was upset by the remark. She stated that in her culture the girth of a husband's thumb was as thick as a rod he could use to beat his wife and the term was a malevolent one.

Obviously, that was not the intention of the phrase's use, nor did anyone else believe it to be. I had never heard of such an institutionalized disregard for people to set a standard for wife beating. I thought to myself *"What kind of a lawless, ignorant and backward place is this person talking about?"* What the woman should have realized was she was now in a safe place and a culture that despises that type of behavior.

She should have taken her current surroundings into consideration. Especially since she felt comfortable enough to bring up the subject to the group in the first place. I also don't know if she were legitimate in her opposition to the phase or if she heard this savagery repeated elsewhere. But a lot of people do get emotionally triggered by various things. Perhaps, too many.

It is not possible to know everything that will upset an individual. How one chooses to respond to their individual thoughts and emotions is up to them. We have all suffered from allowing our minds to pull us into a downward spiral. It's part of being human and that will never change no matter the words we use.

Referring to a chairwoman as simply the _chair_ does not change her gender. Calling a mailman a letter carrier doesn't get me my mail any faster. Changing B.C. or "before Christ" to Before Current Era (BCE) doesn't re-numerate a calendar. Yet if we toe the PC line, we can pat ourselves on the back and say we did some good. Is that all it takes? The fact is nothing has been improved, we simply learned new vernacular.

And this is the danger of political correctness; it hides the true problems which should be addressed. But by placing imaginary checkmarks on our foreheads, or some sort of social stamp of approval, we feel better about the direction the organization is moving while ignoring real issues. For a manager, it is their responsibility to be concerned with what is really happening on your floor. To label a true issue as something else is a liability.

If you have a guy in your department who refers to a female colleague as *"sweet cheeks"* or makes other inappropriate comments or gestures, he doesn't need to be sent to sensitivity training. He needs to be fired! Reeducation will not stop this guy from being a jerk. It will do nothing more than sweep the issue under the rug and the humiliated employee will now feel vulnerable about her position at work.

While we're at it, let's just send everyone on the floor to the same sexual harassment training. Often, this is what occurs rather than singling out the individual Neanderthal. By the time the group enters the training room, everyone knows what happened and why they are there. All this does is create resentment and show leadership to be weak.

But these sorts of corporate mandates are not intended to be punitive anyway. It's simply an attempt to avoid a larger lawsuit. More often than naught there were tell-tale signs of the offender being a jerk but were ignored.

At what point did it become a company's place to change the thinking of an individual anyway? The chauvinist **knew** he was being a hurtful creep. He was that way the day your company hired him. You will never change his way of thinking, nor should you even try.

People can change, but a corporation won't make that transition for them. In this case, the guy is a walking timebomb for a lawsuit, just get rid of him. Equally important, you mustn't let his way of thinking spread or change the morale of the rest of the team.

This is not to say a dissident to emerging social norms should be rude. After all, it is simply more desirable to live in a polite society where people generally get along. But where manners and political correctness diverge is a matter of respect. Manners is about making others feel comfortable. Being "woke" however is about control.

With all that said and done, what should we do to understand how to better interact with someone in a way that does not offend them or cause them embarrassment? There should be a set of cultural norms and rules that guide us in terms of what to expect, right? No, not at all, that's what got us in this mess in the first place. What it takes is an actual one-on-one conversation.

"May I ask…" is generally a good place to start. An honest, yet polite conversation about someone's experience or understanding may give us insight into their perspective. Only seeking their perception will create real empathy. Though, depending on what you ask, there will need to be a certain level of trust to be established first.

Years ago, I worked with a lady from the Middle East. She was pleasant and always seemed to be in a good mood. I appreciate that of my colleagues. If someone on the team did a good job, it was common for me to slap them on the shoulder. I may also shake the hand of a teammate who did me a favor. Yet one day, she politely informed me her culture did not allow her to be touched by men, even innocently.

I could have easily been offended myself for suggesting something other than a platonic gesture, but I saw the concern in her eyes. I knew she felt like she was in a dilemma, one I never intended to put her in, yet there she was. This custom was something new to me, nonetheless, I assumed it had been practiced in other cultures for centuries before I was born. It wasn't about me.

To insist upon my Western custom of shaking hands would be just plain rude on my part and embarrassing for her. I observed her custom of simply waving to each other, not out of a sense of being wokeness, but out of real respect. Respect for an individual, an individual I personally knew. She was still a joy to be around, but now I understood something about my colleague I did not know before.

But political correctness is not about understanding. Rather, it is the enforcement of societal norms that do not necessarily have bearing on a relationship. In the next section, we will discuss establishing those relationships.

To Team or Not to Team

Should everyone be on a team, all the time? It is admirable to want to take a hand in the game. It's a noble aspiration for people to be part of something greater than themselves. A group that will support you and that you will support in return is a shrewd political mechanism. This desire is very compelling for most of us.

Some even say it's a calling or at least a significant part of who they are. After all, *"No man is an island,"* *"Teamwork makes the dream work,"* and *"There is safety in numbers."* But clichés aside, is **everyone** needed on a team, all the time?

Let's face facts, some simply do not play well with others. Perhaps this is out of a lack of social skills or simply a preference while working. In either case, there are those individuals who continually see things through a unique lens and insist there is a better way, despite the intentions of the majority.

The ideas of these contrarians may be good or bad, but how does an individual affect the rest of the workgroup? These people may desire to go beyond the status quo or even the current mission. It's those who find it difficult to articulate their ideas, perhaps because they are introverts or just not able to find the right words.

No matter the situation, their priorities will be different from everyone else. There is a name for these people; *independent contractors*. And there is nothing wrong with that so long as these individuals do not hinder the efforts of others.

Being the lone wolf is not necessarily a flaw in one's personality, he or she simply needs to work alone. And it's not just the malcontents who simply want to upset the applecart out of neurosis or sheer boredom. For those who have worked in similar environments elsewhere, old habits die hard. Like an employee hired from a competing company in the same industry but just can't get in sync with new colleagues. Many in sales are disillusioned when making a switch to a competitor because the process they assumed would be the same, is not. For them, this is not just a learning curve, it's a *re-learning* curve.

Then some simply cannot shake the need to conduct work a certain way or to get on board with everyone else. It may be a developmental issue or just plain stubbornness, but they want to do things their way. And their way might not be wrong, but if it is not in the same direction as the rest of the team, then they are a hindrance, not a help to that team.

Individuals as such can still be utilized, but perhaps in a different area. And yet, for some, it may be possible to show up for a Monday morning huddle, receive their marching orders for the week and have little interaction with others. Of course, this model does not work where there needs to be a good deal of accountability or collaboration.

But more narrowly, let's take a look if a particular organization is the right team for an employee. Just because someone has good communication skills does not mean she will have the same values or priorities as everyone else. Philosophical differences or a desired environment can prevent synergy from forming. Again, this is not necessarily bad, just different. Though, different priorities or understanding in accomplishing a project will impede the productivity of the group.

As I wrote in a previous book; *Avoiding Managerial Mistakes, Missteps & Misunderstandings; The Essential Guide for All Managers*, *"Morale, whether good or bad, stems from leadership"*. That means work conditions will not improve without the guidance of those in power.

Either those in charge have created the current work environment or they have ALLOWED it to develop. In either case, it's not going to be the ideal setting for everyone.

What's questionable is whether an individual can mesh without feeling he is abandoning his principles. Does the team have mores that coalesce with his work ethic and other ideals? Still, some just don't fit in.

In 1987, I joined the U.S. Army to become a Combat Engineer. I'm still not exactly sure what an engineer is, it seemed an awful lot like being an infantry soldier who got to play with dynamite. I went through basic training at Fort Leonard Wood in Missouri. On the first day, I did so many push-ups, my arms were sore for the rest of the week. And my ears were ringing from all the yelling from the drill instructors. But about a month into boot camp, a brand new DI cycled into my unit, Sergeant Wilson.

He was a nice guy... which is what baffled me and my fellow recruits. I believe it left the other sergeants baffled as well. I got the sense the other instructors didn't like him, but I could never know for sure. Instead of screaming his head off at all the recruits, he would simply issue orders in a very normal, almost conversational tone. At times, it even sounded as though he were mumbling. Though, I never heard him say a single curse word, mumbling or not. Profanity was not part of his lexicon.

If he were capable of getting angry, the platoon never knew it! He never got in our faces to snarl with a full set of teeth or to show us his popped veins like the other drill instructors. He was always without any expression whatsoever. His commands were low-key and stoic.

It was only because the other drill instructors were watching me that I ever felt there was a sense of urgency to anything Wilson said. I knew if I didn't step it up into high gear, one of them would lower the boom. If the leadership team was filled with nothing but Sgt. Wilson's, I doubt anything would have been accomplished, at least not with any degree of speed.

He definitely stuck out like a sore thumb. I'm certain had I ever gotten to know him in a more social setting, he would have proven himself to be a nice guy. But then again, how many people envision a nice guy as a drill sergeant in basic training?

Sgt. Wilson was knowledgeable, diligent and set a good example with his uniform and spit-polished boots. If we ever had a question, he would stop what he was doing and give us a straight answer. I appreciated that. But something was just... off.

I believe he would have made a very good leader for a unit full of soldiers who were already out of boot camp and assigned to a permanent duty station. Though the style of leadership he brought to our group was not the dynamic we needed at that time. He was just an odd bird. A nice guy or not, he was a bad fit for the rest of the platoon.

Someone may aspire to hold a particular position or title, but is he the best suited for the job? I discovered long ago, the desire for a promotion or raise is not enough reason to enter management. What is best for the organization is paramount. Yet, I have seen time and time again where one was given a position because he had seniority or time on the job. Or simply because no one else wanted the position.

I can tell you I have seen hundreds of teachers and trainers who had no business instructing others. Though they might have keen insight or a high IQ, they were just plain boring. It does not matter what you know if you are going to put your audience to sleep! It's a big waste of time for the attendees as well as the instructor if new skills aren't conveyed. However, this person might make an excellent curriculum writer or book author. A big part of a team coming together is understanding each other's strengths and weaknesses.

But it's not just a matter of synergy. An employee may be good at what she does but doesn't like the work. At some point, she has to ask, *"Do I belong here?"* It is not an easy question to answer considering the amount of time already spent with an organization. She'll ask what the return on investment for all that expended time is. But one must also consider the opportunity cost of remaining in a fruitless or perhaps depressing job. It may be best to move on.

Where some are fine to tighten a thousand lug bolts all day on an assembly line, others would pull their hair out. Finding a job that brings satisfaction is a key element to high morale and low turnover. Let's delve into what type of work suits an individual best.

The *Work Preference Indicator (WPI)* helps employees identify what tasks they find most fulfilling. It was developed by Harvard faculty members in 1994. Our preference for certain types of work comes from our perspective of what we value most. Those who find daily activities they enjoy are more likely to excel at them, which increases productivity.

Of course, not everyone enjoys doing the same sort of work. That's fortunate for a team environment where everyone has different strengths and contributes different skills. Different perspectives are important. One civil engineer may like to draw up blueprints while another, equally educated, prefers to be the "boots on the ground." Both tasks must be carried out for a bridge to be built.

But which are you? Fill out the following questionnaire to identify the type of work you prefer. This self-assessment is not a personality test that is composed of four quadrants. Rather, it will show you where you prefer to focus your attention.

	A	B	C	D
1	Take action	Plan activities		
2	Take action		Gather facts	
3	Take action			Follow Procedures
4		Plan activities	Gather facts	
5		Plan activities		Follow Procedures
6			Gather facts	Follow Procedures
7	Accomplish tasks	Plan activities		
8	Accomplish tasks		Seek Solutions	
9	Accomplish tasks			Analyze data
		Work with	Seek	

#	A	B	C	D
		others	Solutions	
11		Work with others		Analyze data
12			Seek Solutions	Analyze data
13	Lead the team	Be part of the team		
14	Lead the team		Work individually	
15	Lead the team			Follow a routine
16		Be part of the team	Work individually	
17		Be part of the team		Follow a routine
18			Work individually	Follow a routine
19	Execute the plan	Know the team		
20	Execute the plan		Know why a task is	
21	Execute the plan			Know how to work
22		Know the team	Know why a task is	
23		Know the team		Know how to work
24			Know why a task is	Know how to work

Place a checkmark beside your personal preference.
*Choose the **better** of the two options.*

Total A _____ Total B _____ Total C _____ Total D _____

Now, count the check marks within a column and write the total number at the bottom. Compare which is the highest and the lowest.

Highest total column letter _____

Lowest total column letter _____

The highest total column letter indicates the type of work you prefer to do most often. Here is where you find satisfaction in what you do. It is what motivates you to do well. The following archetypes show the tendencies of that team member.

<u>Column A</u>, the **"Focuser"** (WHAT)

<u>Column B</u>, the **"Relater"** (WHO)

<u>Column C</u>, the **"Inquisitor"** (WHY)

<u>Column D</u>, the **"Operator"** (HOW)

The **Focuser** is motivated by accomplishing tasks. They feel they are being productive by eliminating their workload and other challenges. There is even a little surge of adrenaline when they place a checkmark in the box. These workers like to take initiative and have clear-cut goals.

However, they detest having to do the same job twice. That is a waste of time that slows down the team. It's not as much about accomplishment as it is about moving forward.

The **Relater** thrives off of working with others so long as the team gels well. They tend to consider how their task will affect other people. This archetype is generally positive and hopes to come to a consensus in decision-making.

Sometimes, the Relater does need to be focused on the task at hand. They may forget the priorities of the job and spend too much time building friendships. However, this person is good at including outliers and can spur collaboration.

The big picture person is the **Inquisitor**. He feels he cannot devise a plan for reaching the finish line if he doesn't know where the finish line is. He needs to understand the relationship between the final outcome of a project and how it is in alignment with the company's priorities and values.

This personality wants the rest of the team to see the big picture as well so everyone will be on the same page. The Inquisitor likes to ask questions of management and the rest of the group. Sometimes... that can be annoying. But *"Why are we doing this?"* is a fair question that deserves a response. Just ensure work isn't sacrificed for over-analysis.

The **Operator** likes to know what the parameters are within which he or she works. Winging it isn't an option for them. Following the rules means they will do a job well and not have to repeat it. Many times, they prefer and excel to work alone depending on additional character traits. They are meticulous and make good compliance officers.

The thought is, if a job is worth doing at all, it is worth doing right the first time. This is an especially important quality where regulations, such as fire codes or industry norms are concerned such as accounting are concerned. If the task is not as rigid, however, be sure the Operator knows there is room for flexibility.

The concerns of when and where are typically dictated by management or the project itself. But all four of these team players are necessary for the success of the organization. They bring several points of view but most importantly, different tasks to be done.

A large hardware store or other big-box retailer puts out a memo there will be a change to the dress code. Starting next Monday, all facilities will no longer allow shorts and sandals to be worn at its garden centers just outside the store building. In true corporate policy fashion, the "when and where" may be addressed, but there are still so many questions! Questions derived from different perspectives of the employees. People react to the same plan in different ways.

"Why?" is a good place to start. If you are an Inquisitor, it IS where you will start. In his best-selling book, *Start with Why*, Simon Sinek establishes the importance of allowing everyone, and I mean everyone, in a company to understand the reasoning behind policy changes and other decisions. Without this clarity, you may never be able to get off the dime.

In the scenario of the retailer, it could be a safety concern. After all, there are a lot of scratchy, heavy objects at a garden center that could hurt when dropped. Then again, it could be season is changing and management doesn't want employees taking ill and calling in sick to work. But it could also be the wish for a more professional appearance, we may never know.

So, what should be the proper attire? Is there now a need for steel-toed shoes? The Focuser will want to understand that while the Relator will want to know WHO this applies to. Is it just those in the gardening department? What if workers from inside the building deliver something outside, does this pertain to them as well? Meanwhile, an Operator will wish to realize how management will enforce this policy.

Generally, more information is better than less to avoid confusion. Until these concerns are better understood, productivity could be stifled while employees wrestle with the ambiguity about how to proceed. Whatever the aim, there is no reason for it to be treated like a State secret.

As stated earlier, a preference for a certain type of work comes from our perspective of what is a priority. This is developed by several factors established from our personal set of values. The ability to do a job well and achieve satisfaction from the work is what motivates us to do it even more. It's almost self-validating. THIS is work fulfillment.

Membership Has Its Benefits

Being part of a collective does have its advantages as long as individual creativity isn't stifled. Otherwise, there would be no initiative or innovation. There is a sense of security that comes with knowing the entire responsibility does not rest on the shoulders of just one employee. This removes a lot of the stress when it comes to performing a job.

An accountant generally works alone and is ultimately accountable (hence, the term) for errors in the inventory, bookkeeping or transfers of money. In a large CPA firm, the professional may have the luxury of calling the owner or just walking down the hall to ask a colleague for advice. Though, the scrutiny of the work and responsibility to get it right rests with that one accountant regardless of the advice that was received.

There are several benefits to being part of a team. The first is **teamwork** itself. No sports team expects one player to control the ball all the time. Even the legendary Michael Jordan who actually could carry a team said; *"Talent wins games, but teamwork and intelligence wins championships."* For the long-term success that most organizations desire, everyone must pitch in.

After all, no one expects a financial expert to learn on the job. They have received training in the profession, been tested and have a state license to perform their duties. Learning to handle other people's money as they go, or "winging it", just doesn't spark a lot of confidence from the clientele. But in a group dynamic, it is acceptable, even encouraged to ask for help or a division of the work. Whether it be on an assembly line, in a shop or corporate office, a good team will know to watch after one another.

This creates a certain amount of vulnerability to know what one does is somewhat out in the open. But that's how trust is developed. It is to know if something goes wrong, there's a lifeline. It's part of the camaraderie and what makes a true team function.

Another wonderful by-product of being part of something larger is esprit de corps or the overall **morale** of the people. We have all had jobs we dreaded going into because we didn't see where we fit in, felt underappreciated or just didn't like the work. Perhaps we did not like the management or the other employees. Maybe we hated dealing with customers. Well, here's a news flash, other people probably weren't too thrilled with us either! Pessimism breeds despair and it's hard to like someone who is a constant sourpuss.

A negative atmosphere stifles production. It blocks good communication, kills initiative and even makes people move slower physically. No one wants to come home after a long day at work and feel they left part of their soul there. A toxic environment will also lead to high turnover, requiring those left behind to fill in the gaps. Negativity is contagious and will continue to be so until someone makes a change.

The good news is positiveness also has its influence, though it's probably not quite as contagious. It takes a little more work to build the momentum of good vibes. Many human beings are by nature, fearful and defensive. This is why it is so important to hire good people, as everyone has to work to maintain a good atmosphere.

In a good workplace, people tend to have more energy and yet, are relaxed. This synergy allows for trust to be established. Employees are more collaborative and willing to help one another. There is a sense of true teamwork that drives the organization forward.

Most labor unions today were professional trade guilds a century or more ago, and in many ways, still are. Not only was there the opportunity to learn from a master but other craftsmen on the site could also be observed. As knowledge was transferred to the apprentice, the ambition of learning a trade was in time replaced with pride in one's own work.

This is why long-distance truck drivers of today wear a Teamsters patch, though I suspect most have never actually coached a team of horses. It is a sense of **identity**. It's an expression of professionalism as well as job satisfaction.

Other identifiers such as pins, ball caps or a particular color signal someone as part of the team. The military understands the importance of uniforms. When everyone has dressed alike, there is a feeling of unity for the individual. What we see and surround ourselves with makes an impact on our psyche.

This is exactly why British soldiers were once outfitted in bright red coats. The color of blood. If a fellow soldier was shot, it wouldn't appear to be quite as shocking to his comrades.

This recognition is also important to maintaining good people. Many job applicants come from associates or family members of those who already work for the company. If a friend asks another how it is to work at XYZ Agency, they will hear the unbridled truth very quickly. Thumbs up or thumbs down, no punches will be pulled. It compels team members to discuss openings only with others who would be a good fit.

Don't underestimate the power of a ball cap with a logo. For many, identity is a sense of belonging and even self-worth. Employees themselves want to work for an organization with a good reputation, it adds to their individual feeling of pride. Where one is an unsung hero or suffers from a lack of personal success, that person can share in the triumphs of the group.

A way to ensure the success of a company in an ever-changing world is with **innovation**. Business expert Peter Drucker once stated; *"Because the purpose of business is to create a customer, the business enterprise has two--and* *only two--basic functions: marketing and innovation. Marketing and innovation produce results; all the rest are costs."*

Though that may be oversimplifying things a little bit, Drucker was dead right about the importance of innovation being at the core of what a company does. To outpace the competition, an organization must create and improve. But rarely does just one person have all the great ideas.

Generally, there is a collaboration between two or more people or the inspiration of someone else's efforts that spawns a new idea. As human beings, we tend to think in terms of just one perspective, our own. We also tend to believe that perspective is the right one because, after all, we thought of it!

Thoughts are the children of our imagination and we become attached to them very quickly. It is not until our views are either challenged or improved upon by others that we will look at problems or opportunities in a different light. Without the benefit of others on the team, our imagination becomes stagnant.

Michelangelo's great work of the Statue of David would not have been created had it not been for the work of another master. Several decades before, Donato di Niccolò Bardi, better known as Donatello, sculpted a bronze statue of King David depicted just after he had slain Goliath.

Both men called upon the classic Greek style, but it is Michelangelo's piece that is best known and generally the most revered. It's just another example of an innovator who created and an imitator who improved. Was that improvement made out of inspiration or an attempt to outdo an already notable piece of art?

Did Michelangelo wish to pay homage to his senior or usurp him? Does it matter? Either way, it is humanity that benefits by having more to appreciate. And so it is, with the organization that becomes more efficient and productive through the innovation of joint efforts.

And this is perhaps the most important job of a manager. As we will discuss later, collaboration is an integral part of innovation and growth. It is seeing to it all parts of the machine work together.

One advantage that is of particular interest to an organization's workers and management is that of **efficiency**. When a team truly comes together, its individuals will learn tips, shortcuts and other hacks from one another. These tricks of the trade come from the experiments and failures of others in the group and are passed on. But again, this also goes to having different perspectives.

Should an employee be out sick one day, other members can assist by doing part of her job or at least understand the importance of any potential problem that may arise. The phrase *"That's not my job,"* is never heard within a functioning team. But all too often, siloed people and jobs will allow things, to fall between the cracks and disrupts the workflow. Flexibility is a sign of a successful workgroup.

A benefit for the organization itself is the quality of **production**. The scrutiny of the team as a whole will keep individuals accountable. A certain amount of overlap or cross-training can ensure vital tasks are carried out.

A customer could have a concern that a particular sales representative might not be able to address. This is where calling on the experience of colleagues who have been in similar situations will keep the client satisfied and loyal. And when you're in business, that's what it's all about; keeping customers happy.

Teamwork is important for the success of the organization and its individuals. Job satisfaction will keep good employees for years to come as it provides a stable work environment. But loyalty is a two-way street and individuals also owe the team as a whole.

Obligations Each Member Owes the Team

When one attends college, the student decides on a field of study and maybe joins a club or two. When joining the army, a soldier does so to start a career, earn a college fund or just buy time to figure out life. These people think in terms of an established institution and the resources it provides. The motivation is *"What's in it for me?"* But the team itself has much more of a human element than that of the head office.

There is a perceived truth among human beings; "There is safety in numbers". Though, this probably depends more on the situation, people like to believe they are not alone when it comes to matters of love, their ideas, a professional career, and even personal responsibility. Sometimes, it's a false hope but the desire for that security exists, nonetheless. So, it's human frailty that drives us to be so greedy when we join the crowd.

There is also stability in being part of a team, provided the individuals are pulling their weight. So, it should be a fair question for members of a functioning organization to ask; *"What have you done for me lately?"* Membership in the group is predicated on each member being devoted to that team. Our devotion must go far beyond vocation alone.

Habits and attitudes are contagious, and what is allowed becomes part of the work culture. People behave in ways that are comfortable or secure for them. We bring our personalities to work with us and expose all of those attributes to everyone else. But not everyone is tidy, safety conscious, a good communicator or plans for the long term. So, one must be careful when interacting with others.

Every man or woman has an obligation to his or her team. If one does not consider how their own actions affect others, stability begins to unravel. A careless word or negligent act could create discord within one, then a ripple effect on the entire group. A lack of respect for the body and the individual members will render it dysfunctional.

Each person is to be accountable to the team. This individual responsibility will be judged by others. Waiting for management to make corrections is not proactive and not being an effective part of the whole. Let's discuss what some of the obligations are...

Get Onboard
The first obligation is a willingness to change. When onboarding for a similar job with a new company, we many times assume the process and responsibilities are the same as the employer we just left. Though this is a rational conclusion, it is not always the case. Health and regulatory issues aside, the work might be very different from what

we are used to. It is up to us to figure out the new procedures and implement them.

But change does not come easy to some. Some contend the way things used to be done should still be good enough. But this is a new place with new people and a different culture from where we first learned the job. This might just be good, old-fashioned stubbornness on our part.

Resistance to what the job requires won't win you any friends. A very selfish "But this is the way *I* do it", won't win them over either. When the workload is not being shared or to the standard required, no one will be fooled. More than likely, your colleagues will simply see you as lazy.

But if all the other oars of the boat are moving in one direction, it's your job to move in unison with them. If a decision has been made to follow a chosen course you don't believe to be a good one, it's probably best to put your personal intentions away and move with the team.

Unless it's a matter of safety, of course. There is no sense in being counterproductive because you did not get your way this time. That would only create resentment. You are there to be a help, not a hindrance. After all, that's why they hired you.

Though, it is worth a conversation with the boss to ascertain what if any updates or modifications could be made. It's also worthwhile to note how any changes would affect the workload of other members of the team. A greater understanding of the mechanics of any process and

WHY it is done that way will typically lead to more efficiency and greater production overall. Self-awareness does that.

Get Present

Awareness of how others view us is a good trait to cultivate. We get caught in our thoughts and drift away to a faraway place. During this time, we may not see how we affect others.

This is human and we all do it, but we must be able to quickly come back down to earth. We might dream of the future or live in the past, but the only reality is the here and now. Though, we are easily knocked out of the present tense. This is the equivalent of crossing a busy street with one's eyes closed.

An earlier argument with a family member, or where we will meet up with friends this weekend are compelling events, but not where we are at the moment. They are also not what we are paid to consider. Lashing out at a colleague because your two-year-old was especially terrible that morning does not create esprit de corps.

Most of us would succumb to Spring fever when we were in elementary school, especially if we sat next to a window. Our minds would slip away into a daydream about anything other than the class we were in at the time. And our grades usually suffered for it, too. Now our careers may suffer for much of the same thing.

A fair amount of prioritizing is needed. *"Is this the best use of my time right now?"* and *"How will this impact the rest of the team?"* are great questions to ask to prevent yourself from falling down a time spiral. What may seem pressing or immediate is not always that important.

Being on time, awake and sober makes for a good productive day at work. But at the coffee pot or even in the parking lot at 9:00 am, is not at your station working at 9:00 am. Ideally, one should be accountable as to where they are and at what time, especially if they are paid by the hour.

Not showing up in an appropriate uniform (even if that means a tie) may initiate scorn from the rest of the department who dress the part. Resentment of the company culture won't change it. But a good question to ask is whether you belong in that culture or not. That is not to say anyone is *wrong*, but rather, just not a good fit.

The outward appearance is what others first judge us on. We can argue as to whether that is fair or not, but it is true. This observation is especially true when it comes to the expectations of the whole. Maintain your tools for success, no matter the uniform and whether that be a screwdriver or pen.

Get Skilled

Many employers offer additional training to assist their people in conducting the work. It is important to be abreast of new procedures, techniques and even trends. If one is not current with the latest marketing ideas, that person or firm is not IN marketing at all.

Rarely do things stay the same. Even things that are thought to be well established, such as standard accounting practices, may develop the occasional wrinkle. Government or other industries may move in a different direction, causing professionals to pivot to meet the needs of their clients. Economics, pandemics and other catastrophes may cause a business to take a look at things in another light.

As an employee, it's imperative to stay on top of your game. This will increase your value. Ultimately, it's what the company wants as well to remain competitive. Seminars, workshops, and conferences are a great way to be exposed to new ideas within an industry. Comparing notes with colleagues allows you to see different, perhaps more efficient, ways of conducting your job.

Industry certifications are a great foundation on which to ask for a pay raise or promotion, especially if it means more profit for the corporation. But your company may not have an in-house training professional. But with a little research, you can find upcoming one-day seminars and other events available in your town.

Simply ASK to attend one that may be beneficial for you. Most employers will pay for the workshop as well as your time for the day. Unions may also make it available to attend or provide training themselves.

In a recent survey commissioned by Forbes*, 89% of managers feel the need for more managerial training. Considering most had received NO training at all before their promotion, this isn't hard to believe. But interactive seminars on such power skills as emotional intelligence, customer service, sales, conflict management and interpersonal relations are available too.

There are also a host of trade associations out there for every profession imaginable and probably one that fits your occupation. There's almost everything from notary publics to chemists and everything in between. There's even an association for pet sitters, who knew?

Many of these organizations will have local chapters with monthly meetings. Or at least a trade magazine full of new ideas. It's worth a little research to see how joining a professional group could be of benefit to you.

Get Involved

As we will discuss in the third section, some people are introverts. There is certainly nothing wrong with that. But there is the need to engage with the other members of the team. This necessity is more than just the occasional required business meeting.

Human beings are social. Even the introverts came to realize this during the Covid lockdowns. People want to know they are not alone. They like the idea of reaching out to someone else should they need help. Being a good member of the team means being ready to assist. But you will more than likely need their help one day.

But if a team only sees members holed up in the office or working at their station all day without saying a word, it may be taken as a sign of condescension. If you're missing at the birthday party in the break room, you may be labeled a snob. Now, before you respond with *so what,* realize you might just actually be one.

There is certainly nothing wrong with working diligently. I am not suggesting taking time away from the company when one is on the clock. But relationships are important and are the whole point of people working together in the first place.

If you are someone who is a bit shy or prefers to keep your nose to the grindstone, it is useful to occasionally come up for air on your breaks. Smile and say hello to those on your team. Unfortunately, reserved people are often misunderstood as being callous.

Most public speakers I know, including myself, are introverts. It's not that we don't like people, but we recharge our batteries so to speak, in solitude. For me, I am less concerned with applause while speaking at a conference than knowing I was able to relate to everyone and what they came there for.

Yet, I force myself to deliver the training or a keynote speech. I climb up on that stage or platform and face the crowd. I will also shake hands with people before and stick around to answer questions after. I don't need the attention, though I do want to know my hours of preparation have paid off.

Get Help
Though seeking assistance may sound more self-serving than an obligation to the team, it is not. If you need help, get help. Be prepared to offer it as well. This is how healthy organizations function. People are less impressed with your independence than with accomplishing the mission. Raise your hand and stop slowing down everyone else.

It is the boss's responsibility to make assignments and hold individuals accountable for their completion. But if instructions are vague, it's the workers' responsibility to seek clarity. Too often in business, assumptions are made that waste time and create costly mistakes. Part of a manager's responsibility is to ensure there are good lines of communication. So, if you need more details from your boss, ask.

There are several reasons some are afraid to ask for help. One is for fear of the scrutiny of appearing to not know something in the first place. In other words, people don't want to look "dumb." However, it is far better to look dumb for five minutes than to be ignorant for five years.

And that is the way perception of expertise works. If people generally like you, they will usually forgive the occasional lack of understanding. So don't be intimidated to ask questions.

However, if work is routinely inadequate because you may not know what you are doing, it will cause continual problems for the rest of the team. This will slow production and create resentment. If a concept or process is part of your regular job, you cannot go your entire career faking it. Even those who attempt to do so, never fool anyone.

One more reason people may not ask for help is many don't want to be a bother. When I hear *"I don't want to be a bother"* or *"I hate to ask,"* in one of my seminars the question is generally not a bother at all. Besides, that's why I'm there. I may have the answer that helps solve a problem or can at least offer a different way of looking at the issue to uncover a solution.

Often that response will help others in the room who did not ask but also wanted to know. I've even been known to pose the question or concern to others in the training if I'm stumped. No one person has all the answers, including the experts. So, It's OK to ask.

Yet another cause for not getting help is that of perfection. But perfection is a myth, it doesn't really exist. And if it did, everyone would have a different version of what perfect was. This fantasy only exists in our heads. But personal excellence is only developed through failure.

Sadly, many perfectionists are afraid to allow the rest of the crew to move forward until everything is flawless. But this is less about accomplishing a task and more about the ego of an individual. We tend to want to put our little signature on everything we touch as if to say we were there.

Yet, it has been the killer of good ideas and progress for as long as man has walked the earth. Have you ever had a concept for a new invention but lacked the details to bring it to life? Perhaps you dismissed the idea only to see YOUR creation on the store shelves a couple of years later! Many times, DONE really is better than perfect.

Finally, I have heard others say they will not seek aid or advice from colleagues for fear of being indebted to them. Owing to another the occasional social favor is part of interacting with other human beings. It can be a good thing! Coming to one's aid and seeking it creates a spirit of solidarity and trust.

However, if you are not helpful there will be a disconnect from everyone else. Remember that evaluation question in your last job review that asked; *"Works well with others?"* This is a key consideration when it comes to promotions and pay raises. People will remember the time you put your finger on the side of your nose and yelled *"Not it!"*

But if someone is ultimately opposed to helping others, that individual is either not a team player at all or believes themselves to be in a toxic atmosphere where there is no trust. If the former is the case, a person needs to reevaluate what it is he or she brings to everyone else in the first place. If the latter is true, it is time to reevaluate what the organization brings to its individuals. Life is too short to spend in a dysfunctional work environment. It may be time to move on.

Whether you get credit or not, you should always be ready to come to a colleague's aid. Asking to assist someone who seems to be struggling is a sign of a healthy work environment. This is not to say one needs to be overzealous, of course. But an offer to pitch in is typically appreciated. But helping others is imperative.

Get Positive

As stated previously, attitudes are contagious, especially when working in close proximity. Often, those mindsets spill over the cubicle wall and into the minds of our neighbors. We rely on management to set the tone of our workplace, whether we realize it or not. If that leadership is absent, we look to others for cues as to our mental points of view.

When working with a team, especially a sales force, employees will many times take on the feelings and attitudes of their colleagues. When a company representative calls on a customer, that tone will be set within the first few seconds of a meeting.

A posture of defensiveness will create suspicion in the client. While pessimism may display signs of poor customer service. Being overly jovial will just seem creepy. All things to avoid on a sales call. People take their outlooks with them wherever they go and project them onto others either knowingly or not.

Consider negativity to be a defense mechanism in preparing for the worst. When things go wrong, we can say we were emotionally prepared for the catastrophe. The problem is though, we have that dark cloud hanging over us all day because anything could go wrong at any time. But this defensive posture will consume all of our time and prevent us from seeking solutions or planning for a positive outcome. When we carry the negativity of others or a toxic environment, it stifles our productivity, creativity, and happiness.

This is all the more reason to carry the right frame of mind with you. But this can be a definite challenge around the wrong coworkers. You have to be conscious of who you socialize with because their beliefs will affect yours.

When I was the sales trainer for a RE/MAX office in Tennessee, one of the first things I would ask a new agent to be mindful of was his or her attitude. Knowing how infectious it can be, a negative perspective could kill everyone's productivity. But I was also aware my one, little conversation would not override a lifetime of bad habits.

Defeatist conversations are commonplace, and a positive attitude takes time to cultivate. Many never do. As an attempt to make my concern stick in the minds of these rookie Realtors®, I would relate the disgusting and rather graphic metaphor of "verbal vomit." Verbally vomiting is whenever others feel the need to express all the negativity of the day, or perhaps even their lives, to YOU.

Imagine someone who is sick, perhaps a small child for eating too many sweets. That kid hurls toward you what was once in his stomach, and it's now splattered on your clothes. It's all over your nice shirt, but at least the little tike feels better. What do you do now? Do you wipe yourself off or get a change of clothes? You can't walk around like THIS the rest of the day.

And yet, that's what many people do! THEY carry around that negativity all day and perhaps even spread it to others. Regurgitation is bringing up something that ails us in an attempt to remove the sickness. A lot of people feel better once they vent, but what does that do to the rest of us?

The breakroom can be a petri dish of who didn't get a pay raise, how management is unfair, why the union should go on strike and just general gossip. Everyone regurgitating on one another doesn't solve the issues of the day, it only creates an unhealthy atmosphere. But that adage still holds, misery really does love company.

I would create this repulsive narrative to illustrate in the minds of my real estate team how our personalities can rub off on one another. We have an obligation to our colleagues to be positive around them At the very least, we owe it to keep our negativity to ourselves.

From time to time, I would hear them catching one another down the hall and asking, *"Is that verbal vomit you're speaking right now?"* I thought this metaphor seemed to be a memorable way to make the point of how we influence others on the team. And so, I share it with you.

We devote a lot of our lives to our occupations. On average, a third of our day is in close quarters with our colleagues. Jim Rohn famously stated, *"You are the average of the five people you spend the most time with."* But is that good or that bad? Well, it depends on you! Who are your five people?

I'm not suggesting anyone start a new career or get a divorce because there are negativists everywhere. Escaping every sad sack on the planet just isn't possible. But we do have to assess whether we are currently in the right place. Are we in a toxic environment or are there just a couple of toxic people?

It's easier to identify and avoid those who will not lift us up than it is to change jobs. But we must be conscious about who we allow to affct our thinking. It is our responsibility to protect the six inches between our ears.

By the same coin, we don't have the right to negatively affect the moods of others. Who are we to ruin their day by sharing all the rejections we received on sales calls last week, why our teenagers are brats or how our girlfriend won't give us space? We don't have the authority or permission to bring others down because we want to vent.

It's also a pretty good bet no one cares about your drama anyway. Not all workers care whether you are having a bad day. So, save it for your spouse, after-hours confidant, or bartender. Who are we to "vomit" on members of our team?

As far as my real estate team, I made sure they knew I was there for them if they had a bad day. Yes, sometimes it is necessary to unburden yourself with someone you trust. I had been around the block a time or two myself and already knew how they would feel facing the adversities of real estate. I was there as an emotional support and to offer solutions.

But my experience in business was a far cry from that of new, impressionable agents just beginning theirs. My door was always open, but many never took advantage of emitting their woes to me. And that is fine.

Some CRAVED the drama instead. These are the people I knew the group would have to safeguard itself against. Avoid toxic people and their verbal vomit.

But the majority of individuals on the team had a very positive outlook on themselves and their business. And they would try to help one another when possible. I always appreciated that. To me, those people were indispensable.

The Indispensable Team Member

Avoiding negative attitudes and verbal vomit is just one facet of participating in a positive, productive environment. One needs to look beyond what is written in the job description and how that individual may utilize all their knowledge and God-given talents. And if those talents truly are divine, isn't that why we were put on Earth in the first place?

There is an old saying in theatre; *"There are no small parts, only small actors."* This is an intriguing notion because it expresses an attitude. Attitudes, unlike skills, are easily learned. You simply choose to accept it. Besides, most big stars started as bit players or even extras.

Concerning how some react to circumstances, there are three basic types of people in an organization. Some create, innovate and build. Some limit, dismantle or destroy. Then, some wait to see what happens. The latter group is the largest of the three.

The world needs visionaries who see a bright future. Unlike those who have been institutionalized by systems and policies into one way of thinking, society needs options. People like Elon Musk and Sir Richard Branson are responsible for making others think in terms of possibilities. By sharing their ideas, they tell the rest of us it is alright to dream.

However, there are times when old, archaic institutions need to be torn down, so I will not characterize a dismantling personality as simply negative. Nevertheless, we all know those in society who will shoot down every good idea simply because it's new. These people take comfort in knowing things will always remain the same, even though they rarely do.

To a large extent, this sense of protectionism is also the mentality of those on the sidelines. They just aren't as vocal about it. But when a path forward is shown to be free of pitfalls, they will usually hop on board. They will go along with what everyone else is doing, which is what they have been doing their entire lives.

As human beings, we can easily fall into the trap of maintaining the status quo. We assume there is security in what is familiar. Accepting something new may mean having to learn other skills. We fear a lack of experience may be exposed to others. Even in the name of being a good team player and doing what is expedient for the rest of the group, we go along. But is going along with the status quo always the best course of action?

Years ago, I worked for a large staffing agency. Still, in college, my initial tasks were largely administrative. I had the glorious distinction of being the mail boy. It didn't call for much brain power, but it was an honest, steady part-time job that allowed me some time at the end of my shift to devote to studies. Often, I had an hour or so to get caught up on my studies once everything work-related was organized.

Eventually, I moved to another department for a little more pay. I would now process many of the job requests we received along with four other colleagues. In the mornings, we were each assigned a large stack of rather lengthy applications to ensure those applying were truly qualified for consideration. Wouldn't you know it, I had a bit of time at the end of the day to study. There was quite a lot of time for homework.

I would plow through the stack each day, double-check everything and even make a few calls for verification before forwarding everything on to another department. A few weeks into my new job, one of my new colleagues approached me about the job I was doing. Danny was a retired cop from the Chicago area who moved to Tennessee for a warmer climate.

"Hey, don't show off so much." He said with a smile. *"Give the rest of us the chance to catch up."* Of course, I wasn't showing off but simply moving at what I thought was a methodical pace. My young, naïve self didn't understand why everyone else was processing the paperwork so much slower. I just assumed since I was new, the easier applications were given to me.

Everyone else's workload would magically conclude five minutes before quitting time. So, I offered to help everyone else, but to no avail. They didn't want help, they wanted to look busy rather than **be** busy.

Danny and I had this same conversation a few times. He suspected everyone else would be asked to do more work if I didn't put on the breaks. But once the daily paperwork was done, there wasn't any more work until the next day. I knew this for certain because this was before online applications, and I used to be the mail clerk for that department.

I will admit, I was aloof as to what he was suggesting. After all, who would not want an honest day's work for their pay? I just assumed because Danny was a retired police officer, he would understand the importance of integrity and excellence. Nope, Danny had been institutionalized by a local municipality! In other words, he was trained to think in only one way.

Apparently, the old government agency he worked for had an organizational culture of just doing enough and no more. Though, we may think the sentiment of *"close enough for government work"* only applies to the public sector, we also find it in most private corporations as well. But when the government **is** your team, you are letting it down with such an attitude.

That just wasn't me, so I eventually left that job. It seems those most concerned with an equilibrium of work are those who are most concerned with their own deficiencies. That is to say, people who are lacking in skill, intellect, or work ethic. This balance of effort is just one of the aspects of what many in the workplace now call, *fairness*. But is it ever fair for others to do less than they are capable of?

This Fairness Doctrine, as well as others, is just a way to rob those of their personal excellence. By being equal, fair or the same, we allow those who cannot achieve greater a mythical chance to catch up. In other words, we lower the standards.

But this is a fallacy based on a misunderstanding as to how people work. Many lacking in skill will not attain a higher level of proficiency without training and resources. While some simply don't want to produce more than the minimum requirements, like Danny. And yet, those being hindered in the pursuit of their own excellence will leave the firm.

A collection of lone wolves is not a pack. Too often, people are quick to say *"That's not my job"* when it comes to doing something outside of their normal scope or if another needs assistance. Obviously, these people have never read *How to Win Friends and Influence People.** Otherwise, they would understand we get what we want by giving to others. A self-centric attitude creates an every man out for himself environment and breaks down the team.

The truth is, there can be a great benefit in collecting the unwanted activities of others or at least helping in the short term. Not only does it create goodwill among colleagues and management, but it could help you define your significance to the corporation. Most people only know what they see, and this could be a way of standing in the limelight.

People deserve to be noticed. I am very much in favor of people receiving accolades for their efforts. Notoriety is one of the chief reasons people are motivated to work hard.

If current workload and time are not a hindrance, it may be beneficial to increase one's responsibilities. Doing so could exhibit the value of a worker. When that person inserts themselves in the middle of the workflow, others will grow to depend on that employee.

When I was in the Army, there was a fellow soldier who was the go-to guy for just about anything. As a Combat Engineer, Private Sawyer knew his job and did it well. But he also knew a little about everyone else's job too.

If one of the truck drivers needed help and the motor pool mechanics were busy, Sawyer would be on the spot to look under the hood, even if it wasn't his unit's truck. There was a heavy equipment platoon also attached to our unit. Though it was not a typical skill for an engineer, he knew how to operate every type of bulldozer and excavator.

He stood out and people saw his importance to the platoon. He had our respect. And when it came time for promotions and awards, who do you think got them? Sawyer, and we were rooting for him. Now, who could be jealous of a guy who helped just about everyone in the unit?

My wife is a nationally renowned Librarian. Though it may be difficult to imagine an academic researcher could be a celebrated professional, I assure you she is. She has a prominent blog within that industry and has been asked to speak at several conferences. Hannah is even an author in her own right.

But before she earned a master's in library and information science (MLIS), she worked as an assistant for a prominent college in Nashville. While there, she was always looking for more to do because the work she did was rather easy and therefore, unfulfilling. She considered activities that would elevate her professional profile as well as be beneficial for the school.

She volunteered for special projects and served on committees. If there was a task that was a fit for her job and no one wanted to do it, she would. She ran the monthly patronage reports to track how many students visited the library. It is important to note, there WAS NO such report before she created it, but it became a key performance indicator the staff relied on. My wife had become the go-to gal.

Understand, I am not talking about stepping on other people's toes or stealing recognition. But more often than naught, there are segments of other employees' work they detest. As discussed in a previous chapter, not everyone enjoys fact-gathering or following a routine. If these are things that fit in your wheelhouse, consider taking on the additional tasks.

Different people prefer different things. Several aspects go into an individual's personality as we will discuss. One of the most frustrating characteristics attendees to my workshops ask about is generational differences. Many times, it's a contrast of communication styles.

Way too much attention has been given to group identity, but generational segments are perhaps one of the most legitimate groupings. Unlike economic status or race, the events of our youth really do shape our perception of the world. Understanding other generations will lead to greater collaboration and effectiveness.

Generational Differences

An entire book can be written on the differences between the generations and there are some good ones out there. In this section, we will look at a few of the major differences between the four generations in an attempt to give managers a heads-up on things to watch. Of course, just like there is no stereotypical man or woman, not each individual belonging to a particular generation can be easily pigeonholed into that demography.

I have found people prefer the communication mediums of whatever was popular when they were teenagers. Millennials like to text, Generation X will email, Baby Boomers, are fine with phone or voicemail while the Greatest Generation appreciates face-to-face talking or a handwritten note. Does this mean a manager with a large team must communicate across four different mediums?

Of course not! The team will have to get on the boss's wavelength. However, they do not know to get on it or even what that wavelength is without first being told.

This just comes down to the bare minimum expectations that should be outlined to everyone as being part of their job. All are working toward the same goal or at least should be, yet leadership has to explain what that goal is. Otherwise, everyone will retreat to their comfort zones, refusing to talk to one another.

As human beings, we are shaped by our experiences. Whether good or bad, we formulate morals and set priorities based on what has happened to us. We also strive to learn from our mistakes which motivates us to become better. This very short primer is designed to help you understand those motivations. Just realize, not everyone sees things the same way you may see them.

The Greatest Generation

This group is sometimes referred to as the Silent Generation or the people of the Radio Age. This demographic was dubbed by Tom Brokaw as *"The Greatest Generation"* and I have yet to meet anyone who would dispute that claim. Most today are octogenarians so there are relatively few of these people in the workplace, about 3% according to Pew Research.* Yet, they are still represented and part of the mix.

The individuals of this time tend to resist change, which is nothing short of being human. If a certain process worked ten or twenty years ago, it should still work today. I realize things can and often do change on a dime in the 21st century, but at least their argument is rational. I would not want to compare these sweet people to canines to be taught, but you already know that old saying. Don't expect these people to alter their habits or beliefs, as they can be stubborn. But they are stubborn because quite honestly, stubbornness has worked for them.

This generation lived through the poverty and starvation of the Great Depression. They went on to defeat the Axis Powers in the greatest war the world has ever known. That sort of determination didn't come from one changing his mind philosophically every other day. They were very clear as to how grave the situation of their youth was and they were determined to prevail. No, you're not going to change these people, don't even try.

They are consistent and take great pride in their work. Not having much when they grew up, they still appreciate the little things life has to offer. They are also fiercely loyal to a company. Loyalty isn't a career plan or a good idea, it's a personal principle. They can be a great advocate for the organization and if they like you individually, they will let everyone know it. It is for good reason you may see this generation as greeters in retail stores; they greet everyone with a smile.

Baby Boomers

It is generally accepted these people were born after World War II. The years are 1946 to 1964. They know their parents had a rough time coming up and wanted something better for themselves. Many were born on a farm and made their way to the city or suburbs looking for better opportunities. They wanted to make their mark in the organization and climb that corporate ladder. Nowadays they expect to be appreciated for their experience and rightfully so.

Though they never faced starvation or a Fascist threat, they still had to contend with recession as well as a downturn in the economy in the '70s and '80s. These economic uncertainties lead to corporate layoffs and downsizing. This gave rise to labor disputes. They are team-oriented and have a sense of solidarity. Once they found a company they felt would be around for the long haul and if benefits were good, they stayed there until retirement.

There is a stereotype this group is not tech-savvy or computer literate. That may be the case for many but certainly not all. In the late '80s, desktop computers began appearing in most large businesses. The smart Boomers looked at those machines and realized it was a matter of time before they would be replaced by a computer if they didn't learn how to use it. They were right! There were clenched fists and gritting teeth when IBM developed the desktop PC. But this generation is responsible for where we are today technologically.

Generation X
Gen X-ers grew up in the *"age of excess"* and are used to accumulating as much stuff as they can. Seen as almost greedy by other generations, they simply do not trust large companies or a hierarchy to look out for them. To a great point, they're right! They saw the Berlin Wall fall, not because a Communist bureaucrat had a change of heart, but because the oppression of a large organization failed. They consider themselves to be independent and self-sufficient.

As long as they are meeting sales or production goals, leave them alone. They will push back if they feel they are being micromanaged. Generally, they will take the initiative to solve a problem. This group tends to be highly educated, so don't tell them how to do something if they feel they have already figured it out. Yet, this group is the first one in all of human existence to be open to change. The change just has to make sense.

Having seen many of their parents displaced at work and out of a job for months or even years at a time, pretty much killed any sense of loyalty to an organization. This demographic went a different route. As the name implies, Generation X was looking for a completely different path from that of their parents.

They are still ambitious but not beholding to any one company. An employee who was thought to be settled in after a decade or more might very well leave to work for a competitor. This is something that would be almost unheard of by Baby Boomers.

Millennials

Originally called "Generation Y" after the preceding one, they replaced that moniker with one of their own. These people have never known a world without computers or smartphones and simply consider technology to be part of the human experience. Shoot down one of their ideas with; *"Sorry, we tried that in the past, it just wasn't possible"* and they will return to the work the next day with an app that makes it possible! They are bright, yet impatient. Figure out a way to harness that intellect and they can be a great service to the team.

Millennials are more transient in the workplace than other generations. They are here for a few months or a short number of years and move on. Just get used to that. They like to job hop from one company to the next collecting new talents from one to the next as they trade up. They are climbing the corporate ladder; it's just not YOUR ladder.

Their version of the corporate ladder includes gaining certifications and other transferable skills before moving on. You may even hear in an interview; *"I'm only going to be here for six months or so."* (Pssst, you're not actually supposed to **SAY** that in an interview!)

HR might care about gaps in employment, but the younger generation does not. It's not uncommon for this demographic group to leave college, not necessarily having graduated, work for a year, hike across Europe, work two or three other places for a couple of years, volunteer for the Red Cross, finish their degree, then work somewhere else a few months, all before they're thirty.

They don't care what the person on the other side of the desk thinks of their employment history. They are concerned with leaving their footprint on the world. That's well and good, but not a reason why any business would hire them.

Job-hopping does not create the idea of an experienced worker in the minds of most businesspeople. When joining a new company, everyone else wants to know what YOU the individual brings to the table. "Nothing" will be the answer unless one takes initiative and show how you are helping the team.

That's not to say Millennials are devoid of initiative, though many managers believe this to be the case. For the most part, they have an issue with strategic thinking and long-term planning. They are victims of the "hover parent," and an era where everyone gets a trophy. Unfortunately, this has set them up for dependence and failure.

But whenever I hear managers say; *"I just can't keep Millennials,"* that should be music to their ears. These people are being pursued. If young people feel there are little or no opportunities for advancement, they will leave for greener pastures elsewhere.

They may soon discover the grass is not much greener on the other side of the fence, but by that time they've already left your organization. Keeping the twenty-somethings engaged is critical to keeping them on the team. Each young person should be assessed (even informally) for what he or she knows, then have that ability tapped. I believe many individual talents are underutilized.

If you are an older generation working alongside one of them, they will pick your brain to learn new skills, as they should. But you should be learning from them as well. Ask them how some new technology you do not understand works, and sure enough... they will tell you. Their willingness to share talents is one of their most endearing qualities.

This class of age seeks to make the world a better place by giving of themselves, which is why their work habits seem a bit sporadic compared to their predecessors. They are attempting to attain what Dr. Abraham Maslow called *self-actualization.*

It's where an individual achieves the highest point in life, they can in terms of being most useful to themselves, their family and community. This is both noble and attainable. That is, so long as they keep a clear vision of the end in mind and are not pulled down someone else's path.

Just as Maslow developed the visual chart of the Hierarchy of Needs to be stepping stones to self-improvement, all steps must be touched to get to the top. We are at a unique time in human history where everything we thought would one day be possible is just within our reach. However, if they forget the lessons of those before them, resourcefulness and critical thinking, it could all come crashing down and tech won't help.

And let's be clear about seniority. If you are new, then you are NOT on an equal footing with the owner, the boss or someone with twenty years in. There is a certain amount of truth in the phrase *"you have to pay your dues."* Though, the younger generation may not understand this and give their predecessors the respect they deserve. This is not to say they are typically disrespectful, just not understanding of business hierarchy.

Though they may not actually say that out loud because it might not sound "woke." But honestly, how does anyone realistically expect to have the same years of experience in their first few months on the job? And yet, this is a complaint I hear from managers and other members of teams all the time.

It is delusional to assume a certain level of expertise from a college degree alone. The degree is training wheels and you will never get them off until you have had some real-world encounters beyond classroom theory. In other words, you have to fall off the bike and get your knees skinned and bruised a few times to gain the acceptance you want.

I once facilitated a strategic planning session for a large, billion dollar energy company. The organization was started by one man with one oil well. From there, he put every dollar of earnings back into the purchase of additional rigs. Many were even thought to be dry and useless. There were a lot of risks involved. He spent many days working tirelessly in the hot Texas sun, all the while hoping his efforts would one day pay off.

Those efforts did pay off and now his company has hundreds of wells and hundreds of employees. Many of those new workers have college degrees in geology and engineering. But do you think any of them would have left college to work in the hot Texas sun for decades for something that MIGHT pay off? Probably not! That one man with a well paid his dues and is owed respect for doing so.

By and large, Millennials are very optimistic and love being part of a team where they can contribute. All this excitement leads to impatience, though. Part of that is youth, but part of that is the generation itself. Expect them to be impatient when they are well into their 40s.

We have robots that do our work for us, self-driving cars and communication that is actually out of *Star Trek*. When you can sit on the couch, order something from a department store and it appears on the front porch an hour or so later, we have achieved some sort of technological nirvana. It's no wonder they are so impatient; five minutes to them felt like five hours when I was that age.

Think about it, the information that previously filled an entire library building is now actually at their fingertips. They have never had to wait for much. So, there is a short attention span as compared to that of other generations. Stop trying to make Millennials into Baby Boomers! You will lose.

Instead, utilize them for their skills and energy. Give them deadlines by which you expect a certain amount of work to be done. In this way, they are focused on what to do next and feel a sense of accomplishment when each task is met.

Better yet, assign them a mentor or work partner to serve as a guide and help keep them on track. And they do love to learn. With focus and an understanding of how they contribute, they may achieve self-actualization after all.

Generation Z

There is a lot of speculation about the habits and work ethic of this group. But all that pontification has to be taken with a grain of salt. The reality is, we just don't know yet.

As of the writing of this book, the median of this segment of the population is still in high school. The first of them are just getting into college so we don't know just yet what to expect from them in the workplace. But the way we live and the cultural shifts of the early 2020s will affect them greatly.

106

I rarely listen to predictions, either from Wall Street or a fortune teller. There are just too many unknown variables. But a couple of things to leave an impression on this generation will be politics as well as the Covid-19 pandemic. Those two dynamics affected us all, but they will SHAPE these people. So, I will attempt a few predictions of my own.

A survey conducted by Chapman University* showed that public speaking is no longer the greatest fear among Americans. In the 21st century, fear of politicians ranks number one! Their original research was published before either Senator Bernie Sanders or President Donald Trump announced they were running for the White House, so it's more than likely a fear in general and not partisanship. Gen Z will especially take this to heart.

The two political extremes have left most rational people asking; *"Where are all the Moderates"?* They seem to have faded in the woodwork of both parties until it is time to campaign. But apathy on part of the TRUE Centrists could be the undoing of the greatest nation on earth.

Whether you were a supporter of President Trump or not, he did at least expose just how corrupt Washington truly is. His time in office showed just how much power administrative bureaucrats possess. In a large part, it is due to the apathy aforementioned. The dirty tricks of our national leaders will cause young people to tussle with the extremes.

It could be this group will demand transparency and call for term limits for those who serve in public office. I am very expectant that they will be proactive about society. My thought is this generation will finally call for sanity when they reach the age of majority and can vote.

A worldwide virus will scare the bravest of adults. Imagine what it does to a child in grade school. The need to wash up, lock up, mask up and shut up only perpetuates the fear. When *"following the science"* leads to dead ends and constant policy changes, it feels as though no one has any answers and no one is in charge.

Living through Covid was a time of information, misinformation, information overload, and flat-out lies. It is easy to see how one can become cynical living in a world of uncertainty and distrust. This will be a very skeptical group.

Add to that, kids effectively missing two years of school and socializing, Covid as well as many local governments did a real number on these young people. It is hard to say what the education deficit will be, but they will have to actively work to overcome it. Perhaps many of them will gravitate toward alternate forms of learning.

Due to them missing their friends the communication style of Generation Z will be a lot more interpersonal than we have seen in some time. People will now see the value of leaving electronic devices behind and interacting with fellow humans in person.

They will want their own sense of identity. They won't go by *Generation Z* but will develop their own moniker, much like the Millennials did. I have already heard of Net-ters, Next-ers and Z-ers.

Sanity, skepticism, socializing and a new identity... time will tell. As for my last attempt to see the future, this generation will be nothing at all like the Millennials. That's not good or bad, just different.

A Labor of Love

Though management is sometimes a thankless job, it can be very rewarding if you have the right crew. Hitting key performance indicators or increasing overall productivity is why you are the boss. Also, there is the satisfaction of helping others to succeed in their work.

But it is hard to help others if you are not confident in your own skills. According to Forbes Magazine*, a study issued by CareerBuilder.com states 58% of bosses received no supervisory training when promoted. That's not some to a little training, it's NONE at all! How can American businesses remain competitive in the world when those charged with maintaining the standard have had no instruction themselves?

Meanwhile, the Harvard Business Review * reports the same ratio, fifty-eight percent, of employees would trust a complete stranger over their boss. Is that a coincidence? I don't think it is. With this amount of unpreparedness and distrust, it is truly amazing anything ever gets done at all.

In this section, we uncover some of the fallacies of management as well as how to better connect members of the team. And it's important to connect with the team from a motivational standpoint but also from one of productivity. Every boss has a relationship with her department. But if she is not aware of what that relationship is, it's probably a bad one.

A common concern for well-meaning leaders is to avoid the appearance of favoritism. On the surface, that's good practice as it will bring about bad morale. But there is a distinction between cronyism and devoting time and resources to those who need it most. Being too friendly is something I address in my book: *Avoiding Managerial Mistakes, Missteps and Misunderstandings.* But here, we will take a closer look at favoritism, what it is and what it is not.

There is a cliché or even unspoken understanding that; *"Everyone is to be treated the same."* As equally misguided as this sameness doctrine, is that of taking business advice from clichés in the first place. The thought is if the ideal is strictly adhered to as policy, fairness will abound, and workers will appreciate management's attempt. More often or naught, it creates confusion at the least and the greatest, resentment.

Policies are written or become part of the culture to increase productivity. But when a policy or norm does more harm than good, it needs to be rewritten or completely abolished. Fairness doctrines mandate leadership to

112

abandon common sense, giving the right job to the right person for instance. It turns a boss into a bureaucrat.

What exactly is favoritism? In its purest form, it is a preference of one person to the exclusion of all the others. In short, it's a teacher's pet. Only the leader need not be a grade school teacher, it can be a boss or even a parent.

As foster parents, my wife and I have witnessed this latter relationship all too many times. Perhaps this is most apparent between two siblings of similar age. Favoritism toward a particular child does nothing but create a false sense of reality toward the favored. Meanwhile, the slighted offspring spur a state of resentment and disenfranchisement for much of their lives. This leads to feelings of futility and a lack of will many times.

Most of us would agree; an adult who would express more love to one child over another is simply a bad parent. It's not about love at all, as true love is without conditions or strings attached. So why might a parent create such a dichotomy in the first place? In many situations I have observed, it appears to be due to the favored sibling making life seemingly easier for the **parent**.

In a lesser situation, most of us have experienced this shunning effect from a teacher in our primary education. It could have been a personality conflict or honest miscommunication. In either regard, it left us asking: *"Why me, what did I ever do to you?"* More than likely, we will never have an answer to that question, yet we feel the sting of inequity.

Essentially it goes to self-interest on part of the adult. As stated, it makes for bad parenting, but partiality also goes for making bad management. A team may not be a supervisor's children, though they do seek consideration, appreciation, and support just like children. However, all employees deserve consideration, appreciation, and support.

In a large group, those of us who have experienced it first-hand will observe favoritism is generally more than one single person who has the approval of the leadership. In an organization, it's a partiality toward those who are simply liked by the boss, while everyone else must suffer a bias to work harder, longer and without appreciation. In short, you are either in the club or you are out of the club. Merit, that is to say, appropriate recognition for a job well done, doesn't exist if you have been deemed unworthy for whatever political reason.

Just like the slighted child, they will suffer feelings of resentment and a lack of will. This leads to low morale which leads to a loss of production. A leader sets the overall tone of morale within a team. If that morale is low due to a lack of fairness, the boss has only himself to blame.

If we are all on board with the belief favoritism is bad, then actual partiality should be avoided. So what can a manager do to prevent the appearance of favoritism? For starters, give people a clean slate. Allow them the opportunity to put their best foot forward. In short, stop punishing someone for the transgressions of last year. If you have a shit list, either clean it up or throw it away.

Once I worked for a large organization with several departments. Tucked way back in one of the corners of the basement was a division that held the most transfers from other departments. It was corporate purgatory. The place all the "problem children" were sent to languish. It was a way of easing people out the door instead of outright firing them.

Once a boss I respected for years left the company. I hated to see him go but knew he had some great opportunities elsewhere. Before leaving, he suggested a friend of his for the position. To my surprise, his friend was nothing like my old boss. The new guy was an absolute jerk. I suspect he knew I thought as much. So, guess who got sent to the basement?

On my first day with the new division, I sat down with the manager. He gave me the scoop on what my job was and with whom I would be working. At one point, he asked, *"So, what landed you here?"* He was a nice enough man but rather matter-of-fact. My new boss then showed me around the work area.

Over the next couple of weeks, I got to know my colleagues fairly well. Yes, some were complete duds. Though, many did not have bad attitudes or deserve the stigma of being sent to the corporate holding cell. In many instances, they simply did not get along with their past boss... just like me!

My new supervisor could have assumed I was trouble, but he never did. He gave me the benefit of the doubt until I proved myself one of the duds which of course, never happened. We came to respect each other and my working there wasn't so bad.

Job evaluations are one of the best ways to prevent a perception of bias. So long as workers understand what the requirements are long before it is conducted. It's all there in black and white. But Don't wait until the end of the year to do them. By then the damage is done.

Good straight-forward conversations are also a good way of deflecting a bad perception. If you believe a subordinate has a pessimistic view of work, ask them why. Don't make an assumption. You may uncover a morale issue that affects several on the team and can then address it.

I mentioned merit earlier and how it is the appropriate show of appreciation for work well done. It is the balance of one receiving the notoriety or annual bonus he has earned. So then, what is the fear of being seen as one who has favorites?

Many in power are afraid of this very perception. The fear is that too much attention to certain individuals, perhaps because they require additional coaching, could look like pandering or even sexism. A backlash from others, because one was rewarded for a job well done, is a concern of optics. So, what is the alternative, to not supporting your shining stars? Of course, that would lead to low production and morale from your best and brightest.

Better performers deserve to be lauded for being the fastest on the line, the smartest in the office or the best salesperson that month. I have heard of companies that have suspended their Employee of the Month programs because it might make everyone else, feel bad. The reality is the old saying *"There can only be one number one"* is undeniable.

When you remove a possible reward, you remove personal initiative. Purpose in an individual is vital, and potential is to be cultivated. Today's mediocre may be tomorrow's best.

But here's the thing, those who are not number one in a department... are already aware of it. Most of them knew before any announcement was ever made. But they can still be celebrated for their overall efforts or for making improvements. And they should be!

For those on the bottom tier of performance, a continuance should be questioned. More than likely, they lack the necessary tools to be successful, are just plain lazy or simply a bad fit for the current position. They should be better trained, removed, or repurposed in another department. Not everyone should be in sales.

If someone on the team does not hold up his or her end of the work, there is no need for public accolades, promotions, pay raises or Christmas bonuses. And why should there be? Why would a laggard receive the same consideration as those who work hard? If anything, rewarding those who are inadequate as those who pull their fair share or twice as much, is itself a form of favoritism, for the deficient employees.

Unfortunately, a pervasive and delusional *fairness doctrine* has led to so many workers believing they are TO BE treated the same as everyone else. The reality is, many employees expect it from day one. Why do they believe this? More than likely, it's because someone who never had to be a leader or accomplish a great task told them as much. It's a false notion that has permeated our American business culture.

Taking a one-size-fits-all approach and remaining inflexible does not satisfy the work ethics of those who are other than mediocre. Nor does an indifferent approach eliminate any false rumors of bias. Those who are spiteful will say spiteful things.

What teams need to understand, and leadership must convey, is the importance of an individual receiving the consideration, appreciation, and support that is beneficial to job performance. It is not favoritism to promote the strengths of some and devote more attention to the training and coaching of others.

In short, it is lifting up the entire workgroup based on individual needs. But there is a strong collective voice in the business world insisting on a dumbing down of qualifications in the name of fairness. But the movement of diversity, equity and inclusion can be detrimental to any team.

Diversity and Its Fallacy

"Americans chose a free enterprise system designed to provide a quality of opportunity, not compel a quality of results."
— *Senator Marco Rubio.*

So much fuss is made about not upsetting people these days, one never really gets to know the people on the team. Everybody walks on eggshells trying to not offend anyone. There is an assumption human beings are offended by the same things. It's a one size fits all approach to emotions.

In a politically charged workplace, it can be almost unbearable to go to work in the first place. But have no fear, there are experts who can tell us what our emotions should be. They fill in the gaps and resolve the issues of interacting with others. Isn't it nice to have professionals tell us when we're wrong?

But bad diversity training can be detrimental to an organization. That is to say, of the Diversity, Equity and Inclusion curriculum or commonly referred to simply as, DEI. Of course, there is nothing wrong with any of these traits in and of themselves. All three of these concepts should be present in every team.

But words can be deceiving, especially if they have different definitions from what one assumes. These values are often highjacked by those who have a hidden agenda. There should never be anything hidden, mysterious or confusing about the participation of all members of a team. It is always good to ask questions or probe for clarity when these or any uncertain terms are used.

So, is DEI important? Yes. But "DEI" means different things to different people. Often, there is confusion between what is being stated and what is understood due to similarities in chosen vocabulary.

Is it really necessary to have this type of ambiguity in the workplace, though? Is this by design? Cult leaders know when they control the words, they control the thoughts.

Hundreds of books have been written, terabytes of videos have been uploaded and thousands of hours have been presented on the topic of diversity in the workplace. There is a plethora of information, and from one year to the next much of this material is "updated", "new", or "improved".

The one thing all these types of programs have in common is the money made on the material. There's nothing wrong with that so long as it legitimately solves a problem, and the company gets the value for which it paid. It has its place.

But one has to ask, if these concepts keep changing and being constantly revised, was there ever a solid foundation for them in the first place? If we are to look past color, why do so many talk about seeing it? The practice lacks sincerity.

But sometimes, these fuzzy ideas do more harm than good when there was no real problem at all. The discussion of diversity, equity and inclusion can be a game of semantics. It can be saying one thing yet allowing others to think something else was meant. Consider it marketing, a trick of the mind or just plain propaganda. Whatever you call it, it's not necessarily the whole truth.

Mentalists in Las Vegas know this as *equivoque* or the Magicians Choice. It's giving such vague instructions to a participant that if a predicted object is selected, he can say, "I told you so." Otherwise, the rules of the game keep changing until a desired outcome is reached.

It's a classic scam of "*Heads I win, tails you lose*". The deck is stacked against you all along and the magician can interpret the result however he sees fit. It's this sort of vagueness that leaves people guessing as to what the definitions of words and concepts truly are.

And there are a lot of hypersensitive trainers and resource managers out there as well. For some, it's a racket, while others have drunk the Kool-Aid. Many times, instead of espousing the rules or law, they may attempt to scare people into a particular behavior by presenting the worst possible scenario or pushing guilt.

But why should anyone feel guilty if they never did anything wrong? Because it is a very powerful control device. Just not a very good one.

That is nothing more than manipulation and it usually backfires. Once the individuals learn something imparted in a class was false or part of someone's personal agenda, trust will be lost and everyone is worse off than before. But many of those who are wise to the game will sit there in silence to not rock the boat. But what does this sort of indoctrination do to overall morale?

The concept of diversity as facilitated by some is a political goal. They teach a distortion of what many of us believe dissimilarity should be. But those who tout DEI should realize how difficult the task of creating a team truly is.

Throwing a bunch of people in a room does not create a team. They have to be guided. That's a tough challenge when those people are taught to size up one another's differences. This creates disharmony, all in the name of some sort of fairness.

Diversity training in and of itself does have its place. I conduct workshops on the topic myself. But it's just one portion of what should be a broader team-building curriculum. No one achieves nirvana because they sit through a seminar on the subject.

OF COURSE, there should be diversity! A team that is truly diverse in culture, background and more important, viewpoints is better equipped for success because any challenge which may arise is no longer viewed with just one perspective. This true diversity almost ensures the inspiration of new techniques and systems. It spawns innovation.

If only out of professional courtesy, it is key to hear out the ideas of others in business. Those ideas, which might not have been expressed by people sharing the same background, are brought together like differently shaped puzzle pieces, ever evolving into a final product. No two pieces are ever the same, but all have potential.

Yet so much is made these days about the lack of workforce variety. This is usually from political pundits or those who stand to make a personal gain by preaching a type of virtue. But true diversity does not exist where there is groupthink.

Let's be clear, a variety of different looking people, is not a sign of diverse thought. If a team is made up of different colors, genders, abilities, and ages, yet they all come from the same town and have much the same beliefs and values, all you have done is create an echo chamber devoid of any original thought.

Businesses need innovation to remain competitive. This type of cooperation leads to success in that it prevents shortsightedness and apathy. History has taught us the importance of true diversity.

In the ancient world, Rome was just a small Italian village of mostly grass huts at the time. It was created by two twin brothers. As the story goes, the siblings began the process of bringing the untamed Italian peninsula into civilization. To grow Rome into an actual state, would take the efforts of a lot of people. It would also require new skills.

The call was put out, and sanctuary was granted to any and all convicts, military deserters and escaped slaves who could make it to the tiny settlement. This attracted people from all over the Mediterranean who would seek a better life. With them, they brought expert knowledge in mathematics, engineering, warfare, and the arts.

Aside from the incident of kidnapping women from neighboring Sabine, thousands voluntarily journeyed to the little settlement. Rome wasn't built in a day, but it was built by a collection of diverse citizens.

Rome would learn engineering from the Etruscans, business, and trade from the Phoenicians and of course, Democracy from the Greeks. This coalescence of cultures and sharing of ideas brought about a sort of *world wide web* of knowledge. The Ancient World became more civilized through its people and the information they contributed to it.

Skills and ideas which were previously shrouded in mystery as closely guarded secrets were now all in one place just waiting for society to place those puzzle pieces together. The result was one of the greatest empires the world has ever known. All through the innovation and integration of different cultures.

Actual diversity is truly something to be celebrated. It's a sign of ingenuity, growth, and social maturity. I have heard of several people who are called for a job interview, and then are taken on a tour of the facility. When they see employees working there are pretty much clones of everyone else, they pass on the job. They realize there just isn't going to be any opportunity for growth.

Sadly, there are those today who think being diverse means actually excluding certain people. Consider colleges that give admissions priority based on certain races. Of course, that very practice slights other races. This oxymoronic belief is often touted in the name of social justice or some sort of redistribution.

But neither God, the world, nor modern society owes any of us a distribution of anything. To believe so is a personal pitfall that will shift one's focus away from their success.

Celebrate differences but treat everyone with respect, even if they tend to blend in. But an organization that cannot overcome a fixation on differences, or only sees skin color, will never progress.

Even the idea of affirmative action is effectively dead as a catch-all program of fairness. Over the years, several U.S. State governments have abandoned the practice either in their hiring policies or in college admission. Yet, minorities were not instantly terminated from their jobs the day after a policy change. Nor were any students sent packing. This goes to society having a greater understanding and tolerance of individual differences.

Differences need not be viewed as obstacles, but rather as untapped resources. Former Hewlett-Packard CEO, Carly Fiorina once stated "The highest calling of leadership is to unlock the potential in others". Find what is unique about each member of a team that could be used as an advantage for the whole.

How unfortunate it is smart and skilled people are all too often overlooked because they are viewed only in one capacity. People are complex and it takes a good team leader to see the resources one may bring to the group. It is that diversity of background that gives innovation. But what of equity?

OF COURSE, there should be equity! **If** by that term, we mean providing fair opportunities for each employee to progress. Sadly, even this word has been compromised.

Pundits have latched onto *"equity"* to mean something quite different from what is discussed here. Taking from one to give to another does not create balance, it creates resentment. A resentment that may not be seen on the surface but is present and will erode the efforts of the team.

There is often confusion with the terms; *equality* and *equity*. They certainly sound alike. Many times, these words are used almost interchangeably, but they are not synonymous.

When people talk of equity, they often intend an incorrect definition of "fairness". Unfortunately, that is not what is meant when many use this term today. Is that ignorance, or by design?

For the sake of clarity, we will take a deeper look at both abstracts. But a business owner or manager should invest in getting the most out of individuals.

Annette is a sales manager for the Widget Corporation, which makes and sells... widgets. She has been with the company for several years and gained a lot of experience in that time. Annette and her existing staff are busy these days, very busy.

There is a new line of products that monitor the efficiency of particular machines and are in high demand. Annette finds it necessary to hire some additional representatives due to the popularity of the new widgets which sell for $100 each.

Beth and Charlie both join "Widge-Co" as it's known, and Annette will be their manager. The team has a minimum sales quota of 30 units per sales agent, each week. The sales leader ensures the new rookies understand how the products function and are assigned territories to cover.

In their first week, Beth and Charlie sell forty and twenty-five units respectively. Wanting to treat everyone equally, Annette pays all members of the sales staff a salary of $600 each Friday, regardless of experience or overall sales. She insists this set salary is fair as it reflects the completion of the same workweek for everyone. This is an example of equity, as everyone receives the same compensation.

But Beth notices the discrepancy in the amount of her personal effort versus the same pay as everyone else. The fact that Charlie didn't even hit the thirty-widget minimum yet made just as much, adds insult to injury. She questions just how fair this job truly is and suggests Annette incorporate a compensation system that is more based on success.

The sales manager agrees and implements a commission plan. Let's say, every single unit is sold for $100 to their manufacturing customers. And each widget sold is a 20% commission for that sales rep. The following week, each salesperson goes back to their territory and hits the ground running.

Week two and the rookie sales reps hit the same numbers again. Only now, Charlie gets a check for just $500, a hundred dollars less than the week before. Meanwhile, Beth takes home $800. She is excited about having given herself a "raise". This is an example of equality due to each employee getting what is owed them based on their effort.

Mandating everyone should operate at the same level is to keep the best employees down. It's running a bunch of kids in a race only to give all of them the same participation trophy in the end. All you're doing is training the fastest kid to slow down as she gets nothing for her additional effort.

There is a movement within the business world and the public sector to take resources from one to give to another who is said to be in need. A lack of access is often cited to justify this sort of pilfering. But is it fair to take what one has built and give it to another?

Annette is happy with her ability to achieve a sort of perfect balance of fairness. Do you know who is not happy? Charlie. He states the new system isn't fair because Beth has the choice territory with better customers. And it only took him a short time to start complaining about... access.

In an attempt to make everyone happy, if that's at all possible, the manager takes a portion of Beth's sales territory and gives it to Charlie. Of course, Beth is upset by this. She did nothing to deserve to have any portion of her resources taken from her. Not only does she personally feel slighted, but the loss of those customers will hurt her wallet. She now questions her tenure with Widge-Co. And the teeter-totter is once again upset.

Equilibrium is not necessarily fair or just. And it's possible week three's sales numbers would still be the same. Perhaps Beth is just better at sales, or she has a personality that is more suited to the customers. It could be she knows the products better. Or, maybe she just puts in more effort. In any case, why should she be held back because she is more successful?

Though the words equality and equity sound similar, they do have quite different meanings. Equality is about an opportunity where everyone begins on the same starting line. Whereas the other term is about a guaranteed outcome, despite the effort or investment. So, for those who absolutely insist on using the term "equity", one has to ask what is wrong with using "equality"?

Instead of blindly applying policy and procedures in equal portions, a manager can be instrumental in bringing workers up to the level where they need to be. If the standards are realistic, there should be no need to lower them for everyone else. This goes to identifying the right fit for each member of the team.

So, what can Annette do? Well, for one thing, she needs to stop chasing this elusive concept of fairness. Especially since everyone seems to have their own definition of what fairness is. To be truly fair, everyone would receive the same rewards based on having the same knowledge, talents, and experience making everyone happy. A leader needs to realize that will never happen.

Even twins who are born at the same time and grow up with the same set of experiences will tell you they are vastly different in many ways. There can be different viewpoints on the same events. Perspective colors our understanding of reality. And believe it or not, there is absolutely nothing wrong with that.

The second thing our manager can do is invest in personal excellence. That is to say, giving an individual the tools necessary for him or her to achieve their maximum potential. After all, you cannot ask more of someone than their best.

Excellence is not flawlessness, rather it is achieving individual greatness. It is when someone is doing all he or she can do and is a much more realistic expectation of personal development than that of "equity". But how many times have we seen someone not even try to live up to their best? That's where a good leader can come into play.

Vince Lombardi famously stated; "Perfection is not attainable, but if we chase perfection, we can catch excellence". Considered to be one of the best football coaches in history, Lombardi knew how to get the most out of his men. He understood each athlete's talents as well as his limitations. He had confidence in his players, and they trusted him.

A true sense of being just is less about equality or equity since no two people are truly equal in all skills. But **excellence** is perhaps the best route to merit or individual fairness because each person is judged upon individual capabilities.

Instead of pursuing uniformity, Annette could have sized up the situation better. Beth is simply a salesperson with superior skills. The best thing management can do for her is... absolutely nothing. Leave her and her territory alone. Applaud her achievements, and be available as a support. But let Beth be Beth.

Charlie, however, needs a little more attention. Working one-on-one to analyze where this rep is strong and where he falls short is a good start to coaching him. Recommending a reading list for him to sharpen his skills, training videos, role-playing, and off-site workshops can all be part of the mix to get him up to where he needs to be, which is thirty widget units a week. In short, Annette can provide training to help Charlie find his personal excellence.

Any team captain not willing to invest time and effort in the people he or she supervises, shouldn't be in management in the first place. This is part of the job. But once others see that you value their potential, they feel obligated to work harder. A good leader is someone others want to please.

There is such a thing as fair play, karma or even mercy for those who struggle. Most of us are fine with helping out

others in need so long as it doesn't take away resources from another individual or group. Remember the old saying; "Give a man a fish, he eats for a day, but teach a man how to fish and he eats for a lifetime".
Otherwise, redistribution would simply be theft in the name of fairness. And that's just not... fair.

Have you ever known a hard-working waitress who had to "pool" all the tips at the end of a shift? All servers turn in the tips they received and split them evenly, irrespective of individual effort or the number of customers. If the entire wait staff was a group of five servers, everyone took twenty percent of the tips home.

My daughter once waited tables for a restaurant with a tip pool. She worked tirelessly, though others might not have put in the same effort. At the end of the night, she would bring home significantly less than she collected from her customers. She quit and went to a different restaurant without a tip pool and kept one hundred percent of what she made. Smart girl!

OF COURSE, there should be inclusion! Inclusiveness is a chief function of management. Every employee should feel safe, respected, and welcome. And trust is a very big part of inclusion.

Inclusion requires guidance. Herding the cats, so to speak, means helping people from varied backgrounds to understand where they fit in. People may have been hired for their skills or to fill a position, but everyone's activity must coalesce toward the mission.

Collaboration is the process of people working together to achieve a common goal. It is similar to cooperation. It's teamwork. Innovation and personal excellence mean nothing if they are not brought together.

Human beings tend to only see their perspective of work. The thought is, what one understands and sees is what everyone should as well. Of course, everyone else is thinking the same thing from their viewpoint. Focus on one's work isn't a bad thing but at a point, those puzzle pieces have to come together.

But inclusion is not a ladder to climb rung by rung and one day a flag of solidarity is planted at the apex. Nor is it a group chant or rally. It takes the constant attention of management to ensure everyone remains on the right track.

But that train won't be on any track for long if everyone is siloed or stingy with ideas. According to Gallup*, 70% of the variance in team engagement is determined solely by the manager. This means that a ten minute huddle to ask everyone "What are you working on?" or "What ideas do you have about..." is worth its weight in gold toward productivity.

The best leaders are cognizant of how good communication is their best tool. Is the vision shared with everyone? Does everyone feel safe enough to share their opinions? Are the ideas of **all** team members sought out?

A modern case in point is one of talent sharing within Costco. Several years ago, the retailer began losing money to its competitors which had a strong online presence.

Concerned about its lack of e-commerce, leadership knew it needed to adapt its model to remain relevant.

But hiring an outside consulting firm to build the website would be prolonged and expensive. Not to mention, the external group may not fully understand the corporate culture of Costco. The company is championed for hiring from within.

So, the leadership team started asking around within the corporation as to who might know something about e-commerce and what it would take to get it up and running. Leadership identified a group of employees, all from different backgrounds, and asked them to *"figure it out"*.

And so, they did, completely from scratch. People who had not necessarily worked together before became a team. But there was enough knowledge and experience to accomplish the mission. A mission that no one had anticipated.

This is what I call, *Interior Wisdom*. It's the people who bring additional skills from one workplace to another. Or it could simply be employees' outside interests that prove to be useful to the current organization.

But in the absence of open information, people tend to become paranoid as to what is about to happen. This is especially true if employees sense great changes are about to take place, and no one knows why. This type of secrecy is seen as a deceit on part of management. Any notion of teamwork at this point will be more of an "us versus them" mentality.

Secrecy brings about resentment, and resentment is the killer of collaboration. I have heard several leaders speak of how there is no employee loyalty these days. But loyalty must be earned beyond the paycheck. It is an attachment team members have for the organization.

But without trust, there is no loyalty. Nobody made a blood oath. Why should anyone pledge fealty to others unless they get something in return? Loyalty is a relationship and faith is a bond.

Yes, trust is a two-way street, but it must BEGIN with leadership trusting the rest of the group. Only then will it reciprocate. It is striking how many bosses expect devotion simply because they have a title. No one cares about titles, as the captain of the Titanic would attest had he survived.

Cliques are another roadblock to inclusion. Factions prevent the growth of trust among the rank and file. A segmented team is not a team at all. Openness is not a trait shared by most. We enjoy the company of those who remind us most of ourselves. Familiarity is comfortable but it is also confining.

When I was in Army boot camp at Fort Leonard Wood, Missouri, one of the drill instructors was walking to the barracks one day. Several of us trainees were cleaning the outside of the building when he pulled us to the side. The group of young soldiers was a pretty diverse bunch from all over the country. For whatever reason, Sergeant Valdez wanted to impart some wisdom on the half dozen of us gathered there.

"When you join the US Army, you join one of the largest teams in the world," our drill sergeant said. *"It is true, birds of a feather tend to flock together. And there's nothing wrong with that so long as everyone knows they are all on the same team".*

"But if that team breaks down, the mission is lost and the individuals are in peril", Valdez went on to say. *"If a buddy needs help, it is your duty to help him. And you should feel comfortable in asking anyone else for help yourself".*

I'm not sure why he said that to us then or why it stuck in my brain all these years, but he did have a good point. Go to any function with a dozen people. If there are only two women or another segment of society, they will undoubtedly seek out each other in a matter of minutes. It's natural.

We simply wish to be in the presence of others who remind us of ourselves. Perhaps that's a bit selfish, but if we're being honest, we are all selfish to a degree. Humans are inherently fearful beings, and we believe surrounding ourselves with those who resemble us gives a sense of safety in numbers. That hardly makes us evil, superior or racist.

People who prefer to be with others their age are not agist. For us, it's validation and social acceptance. Though, we should all have respect for, and open dialogue with, all members of the organization irrespective of age.

The ideal of inclusion is more than just a single word, though. It is a goal in and of itself. I wish the people who tout DEI so much, which is typically those NOT in leadership, would realize how difficult the task of creating collaboration truly is when it does not already exist.

Diversity brings us innovation or the pursuit of new ideas. Equity, or <u>excellence</u>, brings us high performance and growth. And as we just saw, inclusion brings us collaboration. But it's the innovation that is born out of collaboration and that ingenuity which gives a company its growth. So, is DEI important? Yes.

The model of diversity I teach is IDEA™; Inclusion, Diversity, Excellence and Autonomy. We have discussed most of this acronym already. Inclusion is not shutting anyone out. Diversity is allowing for a variety of people on a team. Excellence is the personal growth anyone has an equal chance to achieve.

Autonomy is an understanding we are responsible for ourselves and our actions. If one makes a mess, clean it up. Our choices are our own as well as any repercussions of those choices. And the same is true for everyone else.

Autonomy is the acceptance others will have different values from our own. We are each responsible for our own beliefs. Is that such a bad thing?

It is the understanding not everyone will, nor should they, agree with us all the time. Some may not even like us for that matter, and that's alright. Likewise, it should never be mandated we would agree with any individual or group of people just because the group says we should.

We are not responsible to convince others to adopt our personal beliefs. That is their autonomy. And those who feel a need to convert others may give the impression that they lack confidence in their own convictions. It begs the question of how steadfast one is in their beliefs if he relies on others for validation.

As adults, we have had the privilege of going through formative stages such as childhood, adolescence, and even college. Each segment of life has its unique set of experiences that shape our personalities. It's important to recognize that everyone's perspective is different, so not everyone will have the same values.

Of course, this is the reality of the human experience. We all have our own thoughts that are divergent from the ideas of others. Our thoughts are our thoughts, our feelings are our feelings, and our aspirations are ours as well. But that should not be a detriment to a team.

No guilt, no division, no overthinking, no manipulation. If everyone in the room is an adult, there should be no need for any of that. But sadly, there may be more money to be made in putting out fires than preventing them in the first place.

Are you a vegetarian? Congratulations, but I really don't care. I do not want to hear a lecture every time I step foot in the breakroom. I don't want to hear what new statistics you have, because no one is going to care more about my own well-being than I do. If I die of a heart attack due to red meat, that's MY fault.

You found something that works for you and that's great... for **you**. But I am not going to change how I live my life due to your convictions. Just shut up and get back to work.

Conventional DEI training has done such an effective job of dictating what is moral or not, that we tend to dismiss what makes us individuals. We are being trained to stop thinking for ourselves. And after all, that is the intent of much of conventional DEI.

America, and much of the West, have created two political camps. Politicians and activists will do or say almost anything to maintain that division. This is their power grab. It's the Red States versus the Blue States now, but in a couple of years, it could be discord by religious affiliation, schooling or even by age. Is that unity?

Right now, families are looking at where to send their children to college, not based on the degree, but rather the social opinions of a school. There is a legitimate fear progress will be hindered if the student is not in alignment with the professor politically. Is this enlightenment?

Shouldn't institutions of higher learning be teaching truth rather than dogma? Shouldn't all law schools be accepting future prosecutors as well as defenders? Shouldn't a person earn his or her degree and decide how **they** want to use it? This autonomy is what used to be called tolerance.

Shouldn't we simply respect others as individuals? Even if we disagree on religion, politics, or the social issues of the day, we should still be able to work together. After all, that's what any job demands.

Why should anyone have to feel as though they are under a microscope because they are young or old, Christian or Atheist, gay or straight, male or female? But some believe it is their moral duty to coerce others into their particular myopic view of the world.

Though a lot of personal growth does come from the sharing of ideas, philosophical concepts should never be forced on others. At least not in a free society. Our responsibility at work is to be accountable to the organization and its mission.

In the IDEA™ model of diversity, Autonomy is understanding differences without trying to change someone. I do not agree with how the Amish live. Though, that's because I would personally find it unbearable without wifi.

But I have met a few Amish and for the most part, they seem to be happy. As long as they don't try to get me to give up my smartphone, we should be able to get along. So, why are people hung up on the political views, sexual preference or even thoughts of others?

It is well within my rights to refuse to be coerced into saying the sky is green and the grass is blue or forced to address others by certain pronouns. If someone has a particular idea of who they are, that is their autonomy, even if it's contrary to public opinion.

Good for them! But that does not compel me to accept their perspective of how I see them. And that's **my** autonomy.

Someone may not like me as a person, but we still have a job to do. Put all the nonsense aside and simply conduct the task at hand.

But being autonomous does not mean living without rules, or doing what we want when we want. That's not being accountable to management or the team. And we do have an obligation to the organization and its goals.

After all, that's why we are on the job in the first place. But fixations on petty differences shift our focus from what we were hired to do. This does nothing to help the team.

But there is a wonderful sense of liberty in simply being who you are, unapologetically. It is this transparency which allows us to establish trust with others. And trust can many times overcome any differences.

In short, we show up, do our jobs and go home. Not everyone has to be our buddy or deepest confidant. We are free to socialize with clones of ourselves in our own time if we wish. But at work, we need to recognize the majority of our coworkers may not believe as we do in many subject areas. And we need to be comfortable with that.

So much has been made about the importance of DEI, it's hard to go to a business website that doesn't hit the reader over the head with it. They claim the virtues of their hiring practices, the steps they take to impress its importance upon their employees, and what they do for minority communities.

But remember, "diversity" means different things to different people. So many times a lot of damage can be done in the name of the greater good. Ideals will be coerced in the name of virtue only to compel others to think, feel and express themselves in a way that follows a political narrative.

Effective Altruism is an idea much like buying carbon credits to offset an imaginary "footprint" on another part of the planet. The thought is, to commit the evil you want, you have to do a certain amount of good.

Of course, that good comes with a lot of media fanfare. But the general public is not privy to all the bad that has been committed. It's a racket, a social scam.

Both Bernie Madoff and Sam Bankman had their philanthropies. Each gave millions to politicians, which seems pretty evil in and of itself. But they did contribute to environmental causes or medical research. They made very open and well-advertised overtures to help charities just before robbing people of billions.

But do corporate employees thrive in this type of habitat? Do they enjoy coming to work or at least find it engaging? Or, just not resent going to work. Machiavelli would agree, the ends DO justify the means. But people can still smell the bullshit if you stack it high enough.

In 2021, Christopher Rufo a writer for the City Journal exposed training for a prominent American defense contractor. In his article*, Rufo highlights how their employee handbook contains a list of what to say, what not to say and how to identify one's own biases. But this pessimistic view makes the assumption all people are critically flawed.

The alternate verbiage offered by these types of guides is typically confusing and superfluous. Most people begrudge being told what to think, feel or say. Concern about exact phraseology or who might be upset only increases stress levels. You will never bring a team together by giving it a persecution complex.

But this particular pamphlet also mentioned concepts such as "intersectionality", "implicit bias" and "microaggressions". All of these are relatively new terms to the English language and do not seem to have any concrete definitions. It's much like how the term "equity" is used. Could this be pop psychology run amok?

In a letter to the company's CEO, Arkansas Senator, Tom Cotton writes; "*Your company's training repeat aspects of Critical Race Theory, urging employees not to treat each other equally, without regard to race, but "equitably," a term that is often used to justify unequal treatment on the basis of race.*" The Senator then goes on to point out the guide is divisive and appears to violate Title VII of the Civil Rights Act.

But the policy letter also appears to be one of perpetual discontent. In one section, it implies that simply not judging others based on race is itself, an act of conceit. Rather, everyone must participate in acts of social justice reckoning to atone for... whatever. This does seem to divide a company into two groups; oppressors and victims. Hopefully, you are neither.

But that's not a one-off experience. Another contractor held a "re-education camp" for white males so they may expose their culture as a privilege. How is this anything other than divisive if not downright racist?

An entertainment company "challenges" its employees to fill out a checklist of uncomfortable questions on personal matters. And a beverage company provided online training which tells its employees to "be less white". Is this diversity?

In what way does any of this BUILD a team? Obviously, it does not. It is hurtful and erosive to any group of people. All this lopsided analysis does is create awkwardness, distrust, and paranoia. It would be better to encourage good **listening** skills over making others feel they are walking on eggshells in what to say.

Consider how many of these same organizations will hire a celebrity to promote their products, perhaps athletic wear. When the ad campaign kicks into high gear, both parties are well aware the hoodies or sneakers are made halfway around the world with slave labor. You know the ones, those with the best advertising.

But look past the marketing and one may see a different reality. Often, the cadre of executive officers is itself anything but diverse. Of course, there is nothing wrong with that, so long as those high-level positions were filled by the most qualified people. But still, one has to ask why this makeup is so.

Perhaps there is not an adequate pool of well-trained minorities within the organization. If that's the case, the question of WHY begs to be asked. Or at least it should.

Could it be qualified people are simply not trying to climb the company ladder? Again… why? Is the organization not recruiting from historically Black colleges? Why is that? **Why** is just a wonderful question to ask when looking out over the crowd.

None of these oversights are necessarily racist in intent. But many times, those in charge only think in one pattern. Perhaps they drink from the same well that has done right by them in the past. This is why there is a need to be conscious of true inclusion.

It's not about filling a quota, it's about taking a snapshot in time and asking what we could do better. After all, what's good for the goose (employees) is good for the gander (executives). So top-tier leadership should ideally look like the makeup of the rank and file. But in any case, it is about pulling the best out of people.

Allocating resources to their best objectives is a very high-level task for any manager. It's about finding the right fit and understanding not everyone will be able to fill every role with the same amount of success. And there is nothing wrong with that so long as each performs at their optimum and does well. It's as much about attitude and timing as it is training or even natural talent, but all are important.

So, how does a boss discover what is the best fit for everyone? This is first done by taking an assessment (though, not necessarily on paper) of the individual's strengths and weaknesses. Having a good conversation can many times be a good way to catalog an employee's skills and understanding.

Of course, there are professional standards and safety-required tests, and for good reason. But that should not replace sitting down and talking to a team member to better understand their comfort level with all parts of the job. Then, once the manager makes mental or written notes, it's his or her task to help each worker get up to snuff in terms of job performance.

Assessing root causes is an early stage of problem-solving, especially in developing the staff. A boss must see the individual for who he truly is; intellect, skill, attitude, the whole person. However, social norms, political correctness, group identity and over-used personality tests are just some of the noise that is out there polluting a manager's mind.

To guide a team, leadership must be able to cut through all the static and get to understand the potential of each individual. Then, once the manager understands a follower's abilities, it's their task to help the worker get up to snuff in terms of job performance.

But in corporate training; diversity, equity, and inclusion curriculum can do more damage than good. The words sound nice, but what is really being taught? What is the understanding when these words are used? In some cases, the curriculum fosters division and creates resentment among employees.

Not facilitated correctly, some can feel as though they are under a microscope or tokenized. Meanwhile, others could feel marginalized or pushed out simply because they showed up to work that day. That's hardly what could be called "team building".

Another source of division is that of Employee Resource Groups (ERGs). These are said to be "safe places" where people can support others similar to them. These are employee-led support groups for those who share similar traits, such as gender, ethnicity, religious affiliation, lifestyle, or interest. In practice, it is a type of self-segregation. Not diverse, equitable or inclusive.

A better way of team building is acknowledging differences yet focusing on similar goals. Most people want much of the same things: security, financial comfort, personal growth, and a family. Most of those we get from the work we do. This is where our attention should be.

A wise man once stated; "*I have a dream that my four little children will one day live in a nation where they will not be judged by the color of their skin but by the content of their character.*" Martin Luther King knew there was more that united people than separated them. Perhaps it's time we get back to that ideal.

Society needs to stop insisting individuals approve of every new pop culture fad. Let's just respect others for the talent they bring to the workplace without any labels.

The ability to identify where the team falls short and take steps to correct it is where managers are worth their weight in gold. But before we go into development, let's first discuss the importance of a leader's attitude and how it affects others.

Morale – Good or Bad, It Falls on You!

I have often heard managers exclaim *"I treat everyone alike."* If that were true, it would be to not treat anyone well. This is what I call the Sameness Trap. And it destroys morale.

By attempting to manage everyone in the same way, you treat an individual like someone else. Your people will not appreciate your attempt at impartiality because you will only see them as numbers. They will resent you for not appreciating who they are. Let's look at this trap more in detail.

When we speak of a team, we must consider each individual rather than a collective. In the military, soldiers undergo the **exact** same training. They will dress in identical uniforms, follow a set of routines for work and even march in line. This is so each private will understand how another will behave on the battlefield as much as it is for group cohesion.

149

However, this approach does not work well in the civilian world. China tried it with little success. During the *Cultural Revolution* the people of China were mandated to wear the official Chinese Workers' uniform, otherwise known as a "Mao suit." Most were gray, baggy and had four pockets on the front of the shirt.

Mao Zedong himself adapted the drab work suit from another Chinese revolutionary. This dress wear was said to create a sense of national pride and confidence. But as with all things Communist, it was more about politics and social control than it was about being practical.

Unlike an army, the Chinese people did not receive the same training. They weren't privy to most policies or routines nor did not know how each would react in a crisis. They were uniform in clothing only. During this time, the list of what one could not do was longer than what people had the freedom to do.

This hindered innovation but that didn't seem to bother Mao. Everyone looked the same, so they were easier to control without individual identities. But ultimately, no two people are completely alike.

In addition to the dimensions already discussed, consider emotional intelligence, morality, conformity, and neuroticism just to name a few. You have millions of potential personality mixtures. Human beings are unique and should be respected for that uniqueness.

They all have strengths and weaknesses, talents and hang-ups, decisiveness, and apathy. Some will seem very familiar because they are similar to you, while others have nothing in common with you whatsoever. Different doesn't mean bad, it just means different.

Yet, these men and women are all on the same team and must work together. The job of management is to ensure they remain productive and achieve organizational goals. With all these personalities and perceptional differences, who thought it was possible to manage everyone the same in the first place?

And though, treating everyone the same is one of the biggest mistakes new managers, or even seasoned ones for that fact will make. This is an error in leadership because no two people react the same way to any given circumstance. To this end, we need members of a team who are strong in areas where others are weak. This, in turn, will mandate the need for a variety of personalities.

Conversely, when it comes to a group of followers, they are looking for different things in a leader. There are different expectations. A general sense of organizational direction is important but beyond that, cohorts will each prioritize what they feel to be important in a supervisor.

An analytical person will believe a manager should be more bottom-line in defining what is a success. While a creative type will want to be given chances to *explore the possibilities.*" If you have these two very different personalities working in the same position you will, of course, receive two different perspectives on management.

An introvert will think too many meetings are frivolous and lose respect for the team leader. An extrovert will want more face time with the boss and think her rude if she doesn't give it. A seasoned employee will expect to be treated almost as an equal with management while a newbie will want their hand held. Since there is no one personality on any team, it is simply not possible to apply one managerial style to everyone. Avoid the Sameness Trap.

The bottom line is your people are not drones and neither are you. Individuals have different sets of motivators and de-motivators. These individual characteristics must be considered as they will collectively affect overall morale.

If you have a team of nine people, you have nine personality cocktails with which to deal. Finding out what those motivators are and applying them to get the most out of an individual employee is your job as a team leader.

Some may take a dim view of this type of assessment, stating it is too manipulative by nature. But this is not a disingenuous approach. Keep in mind, it is the employee's own motivations and not subjection by the boss that moves an organization forward. So, it is wise to know what those motivators are.

People commit to a company for far more than just a paycheck. Identifying what a team member wants; money, security, personal pride, recognition, loyalty, or esprit de corps is just plain smart. Playing to those drivers is the same as playing to someone's strengths in a particular task. You are finding the right match and that means understanding each employee.

But what of those who consider themselves high achievers? The ones who are motivated simply by the act of doing a job well. Ace sales representatives who work solely on commission, for instance, don't need to consider the consequences of failure. They are all too involved in trying to give themselves a raise by breaking the company sales record.

This may be a different mindset than others in the company who are assured a paycheck. Communicate with that rep in negative terms and you stand to lose one of your star players. An effective manager must understand the perspectives and priorities of each individual.

Treating everyone the same creates mediocracy which forces an individual to play the game. The employee becomes a type of sycophant, saying what they think you want to hear and going through the motions. But playing a political game stifles innovation. It fails to support an individual team member's strengths, which is what they were hired for in the first place.

A more genuine, flexible manager will get more done than one who takes a generic approach. Even the most task-oriented boss can come closer to his goal by taking the time to better understand the subordinate's personality.

Once we better understand what drives the individual members of a team, we can then understand the language of their personality to help that person become more efficient. Now, we can provide the training or even personal development skills needed. The task of raising someone to an acceptable (or better) level of competence will now be that much easier. By creating a better relationship and investing the time to understand our team, one will earn their trust. Continual improvement will lead the team from trust to loyalty.

There is another legitimate concern about not showing favoritism. This misplaced intent sounds like a good way to avoid liability both politically and legally. However, more harm can be done than good. A philosophy of sameness ignores the needs of a particular employee. If you are in a supervisory role, a disregard for certain facts can land you in a lot of hot water both politically and legally.

I have had the good fortune of traveling the county delivering workshops and keynote speeches. Over the years, I have spoken to thousands of businesspeople and heard stories of "depressing" places to work. But is it the facility or the work itself that is so gloomy? Maybe it's the attitude of leadership being repeated by the followers.

Morale, whether good or bad, stems from top leadership. Period! This responsibility lies with the head of the organizational unit whether that be a supervisor for a workgroup, the department manager or the CEO, it falls to the leadership of that division. Even parents tend to say "no" to children way more often than affirm anything positive. This sets the tone for all concerned.

I can walk around a company, visit a few different areas, and after speaking with half a dozen employees, I have a good gauge of that organization's team spirit. There are some easy indicators when morale is bad. People's breathing is shallow, their movement is slow, or their eyes are down looking at the floor. They seldom smile. If staff members notice a guest is present, their smile will only appear after they seem to remind themselves to do so.

Sometimes there are signs, literal signs, reminding people what is acceptable or not like a steady barrage of commands. Posted signs all over the shop reminding people of what to do, as if it were their first day, will breed resentment toward those in charge. Just remember, no micromanaged, unempowered employee ever took initiative.

Morale is usually a pretty good barometer of production. When it's bad, it's contagious. It affects not only the staff but the customers as well. People want a professional and respectful relationship with a business owner. In the age of "quiet quitting" or doing the bare minimum, an entrepreneur needs to understand the mentality of his or her workers.

And that is the point of ensuring good morale. Have you ever met someone who puts on a good front in public, but in their private life, he or she is just plain miserable? Others see right through that façade and the same is true for an organization.

This is especially so when it is the workers who are the primary ambassadors of the company. The sales department and customer service will treat clients with the same attentiveness as the leaders treat them. This can hurt business development and repeat orders.

But there are cues for effective environments as well. The growth of an organization is dependent on the growth of its people. Team members will take the initiative to begin a task without being asked and even go the extra mile in their daily work and with customer service. Employees will have a sense of ownership that can only come from empowerment. The growth of an organization is dependent on the growth of its people.

People want a professional and respectful relationship with their boss. But issuing every edict by way of email is lazy and condescending. A good team environment is based on trust, but not a pretense of everyone being on the same page when they are not. Though trust is a two-way street, it must first be exemplified by the boss. Open and sincere communication is the best way to do that.

Employees deserve the respect which is due to them. That means understanding the motivators of each and that will take an investment in time. Sadly, some leaders do not value realizing what inspires one employee from the others.

A common challenge is with the managers' own time and responsibilities. He has his meetings with superiors, reports that are due, implementation of new programs, etc., etc., etc. But this also gets into his priorities and a sense of what is of greatest importance.

But could the effectiveness and production of his team realistically be lower in significance than all the administrative *stuff?* Probably not. Management is to maintain the status quo. That means keeping the team in the performing phase discussed in Chapter One of this book.

It is the team leader who brings about the esprit de corps. That individual is the glue for group cohesion. It is the unit integrity we spoke of in the first section. He initiates what the connection will be from member to member and individual to the group. But that begins with the respect between manager and subordinate.

All groups need synergy. That is to say; a sense of how an individual works within the organization and a readiness to help one another in a time of need. Understanding how separate players add to the overall dynamic of the whole is paramount for success. It is an issue of trust.

And yet, I have seen, heard of, or met hundreds of so-called leaders who will pit one employee against another. They believe to throw a bone between two dogs will prove who is more aggressive and therefore the better worker.

Let's assume a scenario familiar to American business. There are two potential candidates for just one open managerial slot or other promotion. But instead of relying on interviews or assessments, the puppet master granting the promotion sets one against the other.

If both want the promotion bad enough, they will not showcase their best individual talents or how they are a benefit to the business. Rather they devote energy to destroying one another. I'm opposed to this strategy primarily because it keeps a corporation at the Storming Phase of growth.

Many will point to the adage that the *"cream rises to the top."* Well so do turds, which is why I have long been opposed to using clichés as business plans. But the time and efforts of everyone are wasted.

Promoted sycophants are usually a disaster for everyone involved as this is a sure way to kill morale. What the decision maker should have done was take a good look at the past production of each applicant as a gauge of competence. It should be a system of meritocracy, otherwise, all you do is promote a politician.

And what of the one who misses out? That worker is now demoralized in what was a messy public display of treachery. Pitting one teammate against the other only erodes the very synergy a manager should be trying to build. It's self-destructive and creates more problems than it solves.

This simply goes to bad leadership. Sometimes, the person in power is very aware of how deficient their own people skills truly are. There is probably a fair amount of self-loathing as well. Setting cohorts against one another is just a way of deflecting from how bad leadership is.

It is hard to imagine some are more concerned with instigating sick little power plays than trying to build an institution. But there are power-hungry people in positions of power. It's those who do not fully appreciate their official position and how it affects others.

I have seen this played out time and time again. Someone suffering from acute imposter syndrome, because they ARE an imposter tries to bolster themselves by tearing everyone else down. The hope is all the little minions will be so paranoid about each other, they see the boss as a savior. That's not loyalty, that fear and it's short-lived.

The autocrat may have used treachery to achieve the current status and believe that is still the best way to climb a corporate ladder. For them, it's belief deceit and backstabbing are the only way to remain in control. Stirring the pot only demoralizes the rank and file.

Or it could be a person who learned from a predecessor and simply doesn't know a better management model. Nonetheless, bad leadership leads to bad morale. Which, of course, leads to a lack of initiative and poor production.

Instead, a manager should devote her time to building a positive workplace where communication is open, and members know it's alright to make the occasional mistake. Communication that flows in one direction... is NOT communication. Trust is established by dialogue.

But there are a few easy shifts to make when it comes to changing morale should a leader want. I say easy because they are straightforward. Though, changing oneself is usually an internal struggle.

But change is all about struggle. If a work atmosphere is negative, it will never simply fix itself. Assuring workers, they are a true part of the team who can collaborate or grow otherwise, is the starting point. Trust is just another word for "security".

First, **learn to trust**. In short, drop the paranoia or concern others will take the upper hand on your authority if you show a little vulnerability. Most respond favorably to openness and transparency. Of course, if one does take advantage of an improved work area by slacking off, it may be less of a managerial issue on your part and a personnel issue on the part of the corporation. That guy just may not be a good team player and need to go.

Will you get burnt from time to time? Yes, but it's all part of the process to identify those who are the better employees. Assuming there is supposed to be some sort of perfection on the part of the team or boss, is a false conjecture.

A good manager must be seen as confident and approachable as opposed to paranoid and standoffish. Confidence will be multiplied within the team. Unfortunately, so will psychosis. Open yourself to the team.

Second, **use positive language**. A negative word will spread like wildfire. Though one may think himself a realist, he needs to realize the verbal hills he builds and the holes he digs. A true pragmatist will try to find the good or silver lining in every scenario. Rarely are most situations a calamite without a solution.

Consider the communication patterns of those who have inspired change. "...ask what you can do for your country", "A shining city on a hill", and "I have a dream" are all examples of painting a positive picture of the future. People need a vision of what the future will look like, whether that is a year from now or next Wednesday.

When members of an organization are in a panic due to the latest challenge, they turn to a leader. It should be their boss who rises above the situation. Threats and fear of reprisals only add to the stress. A good boss will alleviate that stress and put her people back on the right path.

Also, **smile more**. A sincere grin is the universal sign of happiness and that everything is alright. Most people do not like their smile. Get over it! It's less about what you think of any crooked or yellowing teeth and more about the subtle message you send to others.

Smiles, like morale, are contagious. It's not just the sanity of everyone in the building affected by the atmosphere, but your own as well. After all, who wants to come to work and be surrounded by a bunch of sourpusses all day long? If you lead, they will eventually follow.

Be open to the contributions of your staff. Shared ideas lead to shared responsibility, which leads to shared ownership. It's a motivator that proves the worth of the troops. This is hugely positive up and down the corporate hierarchy.

Your team is more likely to watch out for your back and make you look good when they know their own skin is in the game. They know when you look good, they all look good. And THAT is a positive culture.

This means maintaining good lines of communication. A team member must know his or her boss is approachable. A good way to do that is to simply be easily approached. Leave the door to your office open and make the rounds from time to time just to if anyone needs your help. This goes back to trust.

There is no need to be the smartest man in the room. Otherwise, why do you have a staff? I have long held, the truly smartest person should NOT be a boss, but rather a valued technician. If everyone assumes the chief is also the resident genius, they will not offer ideas.

Archaic policies should be eliminated. When long-standing rules take precedence over innovation, or even what is practical, there is an organizational problem. And The problem is the team has its hands tied in many situations which will hinder productivity. It's a fallacy to believe all decades-old policies or even cultural norms are still viable.

An overly strict dress code for those who will never interact with a customer is simply constrictive. Even most IBM employees no longer wear suits. Robbing travelers of their frequent flyer miles will only create resentment. And timed bathroom breaks just show the company has hired a bunch of grade-schoolers.

One of the most established institutions in America is the U. S. Navy with its centuries of tradition. And yet, in a stairwell of the Naval Academy in Annapolis, Maryland is a quote that states; "The most dangerous phrase in the language is 'we've always done it this way.'"

This pearl of wisdom was quipped by Rear Admiral Grace Hopper who was an instructor at Annapolis. She was instrumental early on in computer programming. Her thinking was so divergent and so rare, she was viewed as a visionary genius. The admiral was so unique in her perspective, she even had a clock in her office which ran counter-clockwise. Just because.

And yet, the military refused to allow her to retire. She tried several times but kept getting called back to service. She was simply that valuable to the national defense. Regulations had to be changed and laws were passed to keep Hopper in service until the age of almost eighty. Even the conservative U.S. Navy knows when it is time to dispense with antiquated ideas.

It may be time to question some of those sacrosanct ideas. Each rule must be examined on its current and individual merit. There is a false sense of security that age, length, or superfluity will somehow protect against liability.

Something that has been around a long time will not necessarily "stand the test of time." Ten process steps are not always better than three. And wordy documents are no more legal than those which are concise.

Finally, **pour some good thoughts** into your mind. It's easy to find the negative in the world if we have been conditioned all our lives to look for it. Sadly, some people have, if only by society or their actual upbringing. Not everyone has a positive mindset, but if one manages others, one needs to get it!

The world is not necessarily positive or negative, it simply is. And whatever it is today will change by tomorrow. We can take a fatalistic view of the challenges in our way right now, but that will rob us of the energy to grasp the opportunities of tomorrow.

We can train ourselves for a more pragmatic attitude. By reading books or listening to personal development

163

programs, we can file away constructive ideas that make the workplace a better one. But it does take a conscious commitment, especially for those without a positive role model in their lives.

Attending church or spending time with our spiritual faith can be huge for our own attitudes. I am a Christian and unashamed of my faith. It gives me confidence daily knowing I am a child of God. It also reminds me I have redemption when I make social mistakes or royally screwed up a relationship. It's not a "get out of jail card" for offending others, but guilt is a hang-up that holds a lot of us back.

Even an atheist will secretly desire a higher power. You know, a leader who gives us a positive vision of the future. Though, that will never happen if we always take a bleak view of life.

And of course, stop hanging out with negative people! Jim Rohn once said, "You are the average of the five people you spend the most time with." Has this been scientifically proven? No, of course not. But it is good conventional wisdom steeped in reality. So, it may be time to take an inventory of our friends list.

A small investment in optimism on the part of a business owner or those in charge will go a long way. Like a rudder turns a large ship, a little fine-tuning here and there can lead to a better work environment as well as overall production. For those with lagging morale, think of it as a "Plan B" for what has not worked in the past.

In the end, it's always the manager's behavior that determines whether the organization is successful. But can a manager duplicate that successful behavior? This is an important question that will dictate the growth of the organization.

Duplicating Yourself

Whether you are an officer of a large corporation, a small business entrepreneur or a successful manager for someone else's business, it is necessary to set an example. The one in charge must maintain the standard that made the organization profitable in the first place. The best way to do that is to duplicate oneself.

All members of a team must have the mindset and qualities of the leader. The boss cannot be everywhere at once, nor should she try to be. To attempt to do so would de-motivate employees who were essentially being micromanaged. Instead, they should be reminded of the quality of work to be produced.

In my management workshops, I pass around a ball of grey yarn and a pair of scissors to everyone in the room. I ask attendees to cut a piece off that they believe to be a specific length, say three or four feet. Then, I collect all the strands and hold them together for comparison.

Within the bundle of dingy yarn, I will have some cuts that are almost as twice as long as others. Then I place a bright, red rope which I measured at home amidst the bunch. Out of a group of two dozen participants, I might have just two or three who are within an inch of accuracy.

It is easy to see how an "estimate" can go wrong so quickly when strands of yarn can go from less than two feet to over six. That string of crimson sticks out like a cardinal among crows. I use this exercise as a visual representation of how important it is to maintain quality in the workplace.

That red cord **is** the standard because it was a copy of a true measurement. The leader is like that red rope. She maintains the standard for all others to follow. Without her, work will become shoddy, and production, as well as profits, will suffer.

Ultimately, duplicating oneself means training. Delivering a lecture from a scaffold or proclaiming a list of edicts by way of email won't cut it. Many will second guess what is being said and believe they have heard it all before.

Assuming others will fall in line to do what's right is also a recipe for disaster. It is remarkable how many people simply think someone, somewhere will ensure the job gets done and things will magically work out. This is a fantasy without those who know what the standard of work is.

There is a reason why U.S. military veterans are sought out by Fortune 500 companies. They have been well-trained while in the service. Though a civilian job may have different tasks, a vet is going to be quick to call bullshit on shoddy work.

He or she will consult a supervisor, ask questions, or otherwise just figure it out. Unlike my friend Danny from a previous chapter, veterans tend to seek out the right way of doing things. And if things are not completed up to specifications, they will let you know about it.

Everyone who enters one of the branches of the military receives the same training. Though basic training is pretty much a task of just following orders, a soldier will eventually understand the reasoning behind the instruction and anticipate what needs to be done before anyone else says to do so. In short, they take initiative.

And initiative is something that is sorely lacking in our society today. With helicopter parents, online retail, and flexible school schedules, it's no wonder there is a lack of work ethic. We have made the world revolve around us.

For the past few years, Amazon has been tinkering with drone delivery, called Prime Air. You can be sitting on your couch, order the latest "as seen on TV" gadget, and actually have it air-dropped to your location within a couple of hours. We live in an instant world and that has robbed us of initiative.

Delayed gratitude, or anticipation of receiving a reward is what causes us to look toward the future. In that anticipation, we make plans for working with whatever comes next. Automation has made us inert. The rise of artificial intelligence will only make it worse. But we can break away from that stagnation through training.

Good training will allow members of a team to not only grasp corporate expectations, and refine skills, but also aids in learning from one another. Exercises and group activities are times for sharing different perspectives on how work should flow. It brings about a type of positive peer pressure.

In an earlier chapter, personal excellence was discussed. Not everyone can be number one, but we can all be our own best. Workshops and one-on-one coaching are a couple of ways to point a subordinate toward individual mastery.

But beware not every technician, clerk or salesperson will become a star simply by investing time or training with them. In the late 19th century, there was a European by the name of Wilfried Pareto. Born in France, he would earn his degree in Italy, and eventually move to Switzerland. He was an accomplished civil engineer as well as an amateur horticulturist. To this day, Pareto is respected as one who brought the field of economics from abstract philosophy to hard science.

For instance, he noticed peapods in his garden would not bear equal amounts of peas. Though he gave all the plants equal soil, fertilizer and amounts of water, the yield was always uneven. This must have been confounding to an engineer expecting predictable and equitable results.

He further noticed this tenancy would play out in many other situations as well. This was true in nature as well as in society. At the time, only twenty percent of Italians owned approximately eighty percent of the land. His observation of these lopsided outcomes would produce what is known as the *Pareto Principle*.

If Pareto's *"80/20 Rule"* is to remain true, then 80% of the production is to be done by just 20% of the team and vice versa. This is especially true in the world of sales where each member of the team acts independently. But even if one were to look at entire organizations where the individuals do similar work, the results will be very similar.

If a minority of salespeople make the majority of the sales, it's probably because they know just one-fifth of the customers buy four-fifths of the goods and services. Eighty percent of crime is committed in twenty percent of neighborhoods by twenty percent of criminals. Consider your workplace. Is it not one in five people who create four out of five problems?

Of course, this concept isn't universal, but it does pop up quite a lot. I personally believe this "rule" is somewhat flexible. Perhaps a better goal for an organization is to create a 70/30 model. This can be accomplished where a unit is truly acting as a team and its individuals receive the training they need.

So, why not just eliminate the eighty percent of employees and make a company run "lean"? That's a good question, one that financial investors have been asking for years. Instead of diversifying between; stocks, bonds, commodities, real estate trusts and precious metals, why not simply put all your money in the one investment vehicle with the greatest return?

The problem is that markets are always in flux, that's how markets work. In stocks, there has never been a market that has repeated itself from one year to the next. If blue chip stocks or the more established companies were the big earners last year, they won't be THIS year. Better to invest in smaller growth companies or even bonds. But what will be the big winner this year? This is why a responsible investment broker will tell you to remain diversified, as you can never second-guess the market.

Change is prominent in corporations and their people as well. If an organization only devotes time and development to the best employees, the bottom majority pool will cease to grow and never become better. No one can say from one year to the next who will be the star employees.

This is especially true in sales where each month begins a new race to the finish line. Besides, this year's stars might be looking for greener pastures elsewhere if they know how valuable they are. A team is in a constant state of flux.

Let's look closer at a sales force to better understand what may be going on inside the numbers. Granted, there are always going to be those who are motivated go-getters and those who wish to fly just below the radar. But is it only a matter of motivation? Consider corporate benefits for each representative on a sales team.

Often in real estate, when a home seller wants to list their property but does not know a good Realtor® with whom to list, they simply look at other signs on their street. Then, they call that brokerage, but not necessarily a particular agent to book a listing appointment. An agent not familiar with the neighborhood will secure the listing and sell the property. It happens all the time!

Some make things happen because they do the hard work no one else is willing to do. They make cold calls and suffer a lot of rejection. Though, over time, their efforts pay off. Then you have the order takers, who exist solely on the reputation of the company. They usually scoop up the business the go-getters overlooked. It's emotionally safe but not as prosperous. A sales organization needs BOTH for longevity.

Perfection exists largely in our minds. Because it certainly doesn't exist in the real world. And even if one could create the *perfect* workgroup, it would not be viewed by everyone else as such because everyone has a different version of what that is. So, nobody cares whether you have an unattainable goal of achieving perfection.

What's more important than being absolute is a sense of flexibility. Plans will be fouled, and goals will be missed, but with flexibility, you may achieve success. So, consider several options in moving a team forward. There are several ways in which to deliver your message.

Teaching Versus Training
There is a difference. Teaching is the imparting of knowledge. Whereas training is more about developing skills. Think of it as the college where one studies theory, versus attending a vocational or technical school where everything is hands-on. There is a range of facilitations depending on the needs of the organization moving from lectures to seminars, to workshops. Each becomes increasingly more interactive.

A **lecture** is as the word implies; one person is conducting most of the talking. This style is an expository and typical in a school or college setting. It's *teaching* in its truest sense. The participants sit there, are quiet for the most part and take notes. This is largely considered to be boring, but it does have its place.

But we can think back to when we were children being scolded by our parents. We would sit there, shut up and listen while we were being *lectured*. Though it may be appropriate for more technical subject matter, such as a product rollout, it is hard to keep the attention of the audience for any length. If this style of training is to be used, always provide the occasion for questions at the end.

A **workshop**, on the other hand, is much the opposite. Here, the trainer or facilitator will introduce a concept, then provide exercises or topics for small group discussion. The majority of the time is filled with participant interaction. In a two-hour session, the trainer may only speak for less than half an hour. This is what I utilize when helping top leadership with their strategic planning or annual retreats. They're already knowledgeable, that knowledge just needs to be guided.

This format is good for a couple of reasons. First, this is how adults best learn. By offering questionnaires, case studies or activities, you engage the learners by other than auditory means alone. Your typical adult has too many concerns and distractions to sit quietly for an hour or more without something else to engross them.

Second, there is the opportunity to learn from colleagues. This is especially true if there is a mixture of levels of expertise in the room. Where one may question the ideas or the need for training in the first place, another can provide a different perspective. The learning becomes more collaborative. Think of it as positive peer pressure for development.

And a **seminar** is a mixture of the two previous concepts. They are somewhere in between. Ideas are taught, then reinforced with interaction, be it exercises or discussion. This is the typical approach for reinforcing existing concepts such as safety, government regulation, or professional development. Information is given and feedback is solicited.

No matter the teaching style implemented, it is very important to check for understanding at least to some degree. Either through small groups where ideas are shared or questions and answers after each break. The trainer may deliver the best presentations, but if the attendees don't understand or retain, training was a waste of time for everyone.

Coaching Versus Mentoring

In a larger classroom, it is easy to get lost in the shuffle. On a more personal level of imparting knowledge, we get into an environment more confidential in nature. That is to say, those coached are more willing to ask questions and bare their vulnerability due to the relationship that has been created.

Individual attention shines the spotlight on the student and that student feels more compelled to take advantage of the learning opportunity given. They also tend to seek out information in a way that fits their specific learning style.

Coaching is working in small groups or even rotating individually with just a handful of trainees at any given week or month. This is usually set for a specific length of time. Coaching has a set of goals to be accomplished by the end of the program.

The team leader may provide this training but doesn't have to. More than likely, we have all been in the position of the new guy or gal and need to be shown the ropes. This could be a formal intake orientation run by a Personnel Department or the casual shadowing of a senior worker for a few days. In either case, it is good for a manager to touch base occasionally with the new hire.

And yet, there will be times the boss must bring an existing employee up to speed. This could be to learn an improved process or new machinery. Again, this should be for a certain amount of time and expectations of proficiency should be established in the beginning.

Counseling can also operate in such a fashion, but the outcome is more toward acceptance of personal limitations or even something tragic. This can get emotionally messy very fast! And though managers do sometimes feel they are therapists, it is not an avenue we will study here.

If one is not a licensed therapist, this peeling back of emotional layers should be avoided. If you suspect someone would benefit from counseling, speak with your Human Resources Director.

On the other hand, **mentoring** can be quite rewarding. It's instrumental for both parties. Though a coach may have two or three pupils, a mentor will typically focus attention on only one at a time.

Both styles of instruction are individual, but mentoring is more personal. This is much like the arrangement of Socrates with his pupil Plato. And then from Plato to Aristotle to whom all knowledge was imparted.

The one dispersing their wisdom is the mentor. The benefactor is the protégé or apprentice. It's an intimate relationship built on trust. It is grooming one for the future. We see this in family businesses where the child grows up within the organization and will one day take the helm as president or CEO.

You will many times see this play out informally as one reaches retirement age. After all, why let the advantage of all that experience go to waste? People don't want a gold watch; they want to know their efforts meant something. They want to create a legacy and the protégé does that.

There is no timeframe for this arrangement as it is an actual relationship. Many times, a relationship will go years beyond retirement or even after one moves to another company. For that matter, a mentor and an apprentice don't need to be from the same company or even industry. It's about seeking help and giving help.

When I was in college, the faculty advisor of my Fraternity was Dr. Ralph Hillman. He taught a Voice and Diction Class as well as several other communications courses. Though I never took one of his classes, I remember him visiting us and sharing lessons on time management or other subjects.

I am fortunate I was able to reconnect with him a few years before his passing. He introduced me to several books and new ideas. Even after his retirement, he wanted to keep up with changing trends and he seemed to be ahead of the curve. We met several times, or through online correspondence and I would pick his brain about public speaking. I am a better speaker today for the knowledge he shared.

Corporate management is not on the hook for directly providing coaching, mentoring or even training for that matter. But it is on the hook for getting people the tools necessary for team success and individual excellence. Mentoring can be sanctioned as an official program or informally adopted in smaller organizations.

But when it comes to helping others to excel, you want to be certain the right guides are in place. Otherwise, more damage can be done than good. Apprenticeships can be like morale, as we discussed in the previous chapter; good or bad, it falls back on you.

So, what would make a good mentor? Perhaps one of the greatest characteristics is having the heart of a teacher. That is to say; patience. What a senior employee may take as second nature, a new worker might mess up several times. This has to be expected and tolerated to a degree.

Remember, experience comes in part from making mistakes and these mistakes are probably similar to the ones made by the teacher back in the day. But even if that is not the case, people all learn in different ways and at different levels.

A directive as simple as *"get the team some coffee"* is filled with challenges. The newbie's head can be filled with questions such as; Where do I get coffee? From the breakroom or a coffee shop on the corner? Which corner? Should I ask everyone how they take their coffee? Who pays? Do I have to pay because I'm new? Will I be reimbursed? How much is "some"? The concerns and their variables are ridiculously endless.

So, relatively simple tasks will be fouled up from time to time. But one great characteristic to exemplify is that of patience. People tend to make a mess of things when they are under pressure and frustrated. It is not the job of the mentor to be the boss, but simply a guide.

Be certain to select someone who is focused on the apprentice. Far too often I will see a mentor take someone under his wings if for no other reason than to have someone to talk to. They will wax on, not so eloquently, about how things were in the old days and how things should be that way now.

The apprentice will pick up habits, because… that's what they are supposed to do. Rambling on is a trait you do not want to perpetuate. Neither is a bad attitude. Never select a guide for a younger employee because they seemingly have nothing better to do. You will only create a negative, rambling clone. And now you have two of them to deal with.

Never assign a protégé to someone reluctant to work with the person. Not at least, unless it is understood on the front end, that coaching, or mentoring is part of the job for which they were hired. A manager may think everything will smooth out once they start working together. Maybe, and maybe not. Not everyone is cut out for this sort of thing. In fact, most people aren't.

A mentor must have good communication skills. This doesn't just mean talking but speaking the mental language of the apprentice. Everyone thinks differently, based on experience, emotions and quite honestly what they want to hear. To understand the thoughts of another involves getting in that person's head to an extent that can only come from truly listening.

It also includes the ability to be blunt, which will be required from time to time. As mentioned earlier, one difference between the coach and the mentor is the relationship of trust. A coach may be blunt simply because it is what's required. Whereas a mentor may say much the same thing, the student knows it is for his or her own good and what they need to hear. That type of reaction only comes from trust.

A good mentor need not be significantly older than the protégé. Though this may be helpful to establish respect initially. They don't need to be the same gender or even from the same department of the organization. What is required is a willingness to help others.

Finally, the mentor needs to be technically proficient. It's important the trainee see themselves in a few years where the senior employee is now. *"Do as I do or say"* only goes so far. People need to see what success is as well as a path to it. Exhibiting proficiency is motivational for one to achieve excellence.

This characteristic is being discussed last because technical skills, though important, are not as important as people skills. At least, not when it comes to mentoring. Communication is key and highlighting the little achievements of trainees goes a long way in adding to their own proficiency.

So many times, people do not realize how far they have come unless it is pointed out. They learn things that become second nature to them. Much like the mentor back in the day.

I have conducted women's conferences for several years. On many occasions, I have heard frustrated businesswomen state how hard it is to locate female professionals who are willing to be mentors. I mention this because it is unfortunately a learning gap in American training. This phenomenon is written about in Cheryl Sandberg's best-selling book *Lean In*. *

At first glance, it may seem easy to size up an employee. Much attention has been made lately to the various behavioral assessments. They are all the rage in the corporate world.

We tend to assess people by extremes: rich or poor, young or old, educated or not. People are far more complex than a simple X/Y chart, however. Consider learning styles or the pursuit of pleasure versus an aversion to pain. A personality is the sum of several dynamics, plus experience and perspective.

Though a useful tool, these *personality tests* don't paint a complete picture. Nor do they define a root cause or motivation. In the observation of cause and effect, they only describe the effect of behaviors and not WHY someone is inclined to act in a particular way.

It may not be any of our business as to why a person is the way he or she is in the first place. Unless that person creates a disruption from the work or with others, of course. And this is why I believe so many in leadership consider personality tests to be so essential. The C Suite is looking for answers.

I sometimes utilize these tools in my workshops and will do so when asked. Generally, people find them fun to do. It is engaging to see people compare notes with one another, even those who feel the results were wrong.

But they are perhaps most beneficial to the person who is answering the questionnaire. Those who are heavily task-oriented may have an epiphany as to how much of a taskmaster they are at work. A little bit of self-awareness goes a long way.

A good manager will resist the temptation to place team members into boxes or pigeonholes. Otherwise, how would anyone lacking in personal development ever improve? People are far more complex than a personality assessment.

It is also fair to acknowledge many will take on slightly different personas at work than at home or with friends. That shy bookkeeper in Accounting may be a diehard Metallica fan. One size does not fit all when it comes to dealing with human beings.

If you're in management, the job IS dealing with human beings. Products, services and processes are important, but it all falls apart without the group. It is tempting to view the team from a collective standpoint; that which is the organization as a whole. But within that chain are several links, all with different perspectives themselves.

The trick to managing several people at one time is to understand what motivates each individual member of a team. If one supervises a large group, that sounds challenging, and it is. But again, this is management!

It is fair and should be obvious to say no two people are exactly alike, no matter how much we may wish others were like us. With so many variables to how an individual behaves, we have to take the at-work persona with a grain of salt. But what we see in the workplace, could be somewhat or even very different in a private setting at home.

This does not necessarily mean people are putting on a public façade, however. It could just be people exhibit more of the talent, intellect and personal approach needed to accomplish the job. These *chameleons* are adapting to the circumstance of attaining a goal, and there is nothing wrong with that.

One of the most widely used personality systems is DISC. These are the four quadrants of those who are said to be **D**ominant, **I**nfluential, **S**teady and **C**onscientious. It is where the task orientation we spoke of in the previous chapter intersects with the severity of extroversion.

Several variations have manifested using colors and animals. I am certain one could be made illustrated by the Beatles. But none of this is new.

The first personality test was developed thousands of years ago. The famed Greek physician Hippocrates was a keen observer of his patients and human beings in general. He would diagnose a person's fluid to ascertain what was ailing the patient.

In studying one's bile, Hippocrates would note its brightness. If it were a certain color, the one being observed was said to be <u>Choleric</u> or abrupt and forceful. But if saliva was a certain way, that individual would be deemed <u>Phlegmatic</u>. That is to say, calm and cool-headed.

The brain fluid or *black bile* of a <u>Melancholic</u> would not be observed until after death but was said to explain why the deceased was so reserved or even depressed. While someone who was perceived as <u>Sanguine</u> was said to have good blood. These were "diagnosed" by their outgoing personalities and optimism.

Though this smacks in the face of medicine today, Hippocrates was on to something. Fluids aside, he discovered personalities can be identified across two dimensions, though he probably never used an X/Y chart. The Choleric, Sanguine, Phlegmatic and Melancholic fall in line with the D-I-S-C of today respectively. The point is, none of this is new.

The Myers-Briggs test is an extension of DISC. Though, its four quadrants are further divided allowing for greater detail. It contains sixteen archetypes instead of just four. But it is essentially the same concept.

I know of a CEO who has all of his employees complete these self-evaluations. It is company policy to have that personality type posted on little cards within everyone's office, cubicle, or workstation. The idea is to notify anyone visiting as to what type of person they are talking to.

However, I find this practice demeaning. This type of pigeonholing does not allow for the recognition of an individual personality. They're just another subset of the collective. With that comes the temptation of second-guessing how someone may act or feel.

Don't get me wrong, these assessments can be important tools, but they are not the only ones. They can be indicators of work preferences. Not a whole person.

Dealing with archetypes is intended to be a guide, not a solution in and of itself. No relationship is created because assumptions are made. Maybe someone just doesn't feel very "Dominant" that day. It happens.

As discussed earlier, humans are so much more than the intersection of just two dimensions. Though it is good to

185

understand a particular communication style, we need to invest the effort to understand the entire person. This is especially true as the team leader.

Connections take time. At least longer than it takes to read a flashcard with an archetype on it. Trust is initiated by the superior, not the other way around. So, just take these personality test as a resource on where to begin.

There may seem to be an epiphany for some as extroverts are thought to be more outgoing and therefore better salespeople. But perhaps an extrovert is an accountant because she really enjoys working with numbers and is a party animal on the weekend.

Again, let's not stereotype or pigeonhole anyone. Nor should these tools be utilized as a substitute for having an actual relationship with a subordinate. Respect is built on the foundation of trust and that takes time.

Good training is about imparting the skills our team needs. But we cannot expect to do well unless we set a good example for them. Training as well as feedback, are about ensuring the standards are maintained.

Maintaining the Standard

Life is a series of us getting off track. What is important is we get back on track. Feedback allows others the ability to make course corrections.

It has been said passenger flights are off course to their destination ninety percent of the time if not more. It may only be on course during the instants when it's crossing from off-course in one direction to off-course in another other direction. A pilot simply needs to keep an eye on the instruments and make the appropriate adjustments.

But the passengers hardly ever know the difference. Turbulence is not typically fatal. And not all course corrections need to be a massive shift. A one-degree change can be a lot if it gets you to your destination.

Employee evaluations are another way to ensure duplication of standards. It helps keep people on course. Without evaluations, members of a team are flying blind. Everyone appreciates the occasional praise for a job well done, but that in and of itself doesn't always provide the long-term guidance needed.

Employee evaluations and the accompanying interviews provide an opportunity for managers to assess a worker's performance and provide feedback on areas that may need improvement. But this is also a time to recognize improvements, contributions and personal achievements as well.

There are a lot of bad practices when it comes to performance reviews in American business. Perhaps most critical, there is a misunderstanding as to what reviews are intended to be. Another negative habit is the absence of a logical process for its facilitation. Third, there is the frequency or lack thereof.

Those being evaluated should not feel a sense of dread during "evaluation week". But all three of the above-mentioned pitfalls give personnel up and down the corporate ladder feelings of impending doom. But it's not doom, far from it. It's an opportunity for some good, interpersonal communication.

I have heard of and seen several in power who use reviews as a time to "stick it" to contrarian employees. It's as though they keep a journal for several months of every minor infraction awaiting the right time to unload. That would put the focus on the boss, and not the worker.

Without good communication all along, a boss can wonder why someone consistently tardy would not know the importance of being on time. Meanwhile, the fellow who always arrives fifteen minutes late but puts in a good day's work, never knows there is an issue. One is resentful, and the other is oblivious because of poor communication.

It's a conversation for everyone across the board, not just those in need of "fixing". Attention should be given to the employee's strengths, weaknesses and improvements. Though the working relationship between superior and subordinate will naturally come into the discussion, this is not a bitch session for management.

This is also not a time for correcting what should be addressed on an immediate basis. If a staffer consistently makes a costly mistake, it should be brought to their attention the day it is discovered. Otherwise, a pattern of substandard productivity could develop.

Conducting effective employee evals is a critical skill for managers, as it provides opportunities for guidance and correction. Yet, it can also improve employee engagement, retention, and overall productivity. But all too often, this time is viewed as a one-way street by management as well as team members.

But this is not a monologue. The worker should also have a voice as to how effective they believe themselves to be. When implemented the right way, these conversations should be positive ones as that is what they are meant to be.

And that means listening to what that team member has to say. Good, active listening will many times uncover an issue that was previously unnoticed.

So, what exactly is an evaluation? The purpose of a job performance review program should be to create a routine of providing that good, interpersonal communication. It's a pause in our daily work lives, but it is also an investment in our employees.

Not everyone will mesh on a personal level and that's alright. Leave personality, politics and philosophy out of it if they do not affect the job. We want a dialogue about effectiveness, and how to improve it.

Perhaps a good place to start is with his or her technical skills. If this is work in a shop, what does their production look like? Are the needed skills present? In sales, production numbers will also be looked at. An assembly line stoppage is costly. Has the worker been responsible for that? If so, what was the cause and frequency?

What are the key performance indicators, or KPIs? Units made, sales records and customer satisfaction surveys can all go into the mix. A KPI is a wonderful measuring stick because it is an objective analysis. This helps a boss focus on the work behavior, not the personality. There's nothing personal about numbers.

Just know where those metrics come from. Are they based on personal production, compared to the rest of the department, an industry standard or completely arbitrary? Who set these measurements and MOST important, is the employee familiar with them?

You cannot hold someone accountable for what they do not know. No one can make improvements unless they understand the metrics and where they fall in them. If someone does not understand the parameters by which they work, that is a failure of management, not staff.

In college, I had a finance professor who did not grade on a typical letter scale. He used stars and black holes. Though, I believe the occasional comet came into play as well. At midterms, I asked him how my grades looked because obviously, I had no idea. He told me I was leading by three stars.

What the hell does that mean?!? All I know is my transcript does not have any cosmic signs on it. And I could have done better if I knew where I was in the first place.

In addition to the numbers, communicate an individual's contribution to the team as a whole. This is the "Works well with others" portion of most evaluation forms. Are they siloed when they need to interact and collaborate? What is their relationship with other employees?

Were goals set at the last review? If so, did they meet them? Why or why not? What goals should be set now?

No one should fly blind when it comes to their job. Is a member of the team on a path to dismissal? If so, why? If someone is on the bubble, don't sugarcoat it, speak to them directly.

Otherwise, you will be blamed for poor management if that bubble pops. And most would be inclined to agree with the one terminated. As the one in charge, you owe it to them to shoot straight in your communication style. One doesn't have to be rude, but a review is the best time for being plain-spoken.

In terms of the facilitation of performance reviews, this is another area where business tends to get it wrong. It's a process that should be conducted in three parts. The report itself should be written and then delivered in person as a discussion of all the major points. In many cases, there will be a need to follow up on those points.

Ideally, there will be a standard form used by a Human Resource department or a generic one for your industry. If not, there are hundreds of templates on the internet. Though, I believe anything beyond a page or two is a waste of time.

Just remember, if this form is the rulebook for the game, the employee should know what those rules are long before the game is played. Nothing about a performance review should be a surprise. In fact, they should be given or emailed a copy of the form when they onboard.

Once a review form is written, the ideas on it need to be imparted to that person... **IN** person. The subject must be interviewed to offer a chance to agree or challenge anything stated. Both should work together to establish goals for moving forward.

A manager needs to prepare in advance and set aside enough time to conduct a thorough conversation. The interview should be conducted in a private and comfortable setting, such as an unused conference room or the manager's office. To listen intently, the counterpart needs to feel comfortable.

Set the tone for the meeting and establish a positive and constructive environment. Explain the purpose of the evaluation and that it is based on observations during a particular period. It's not the judgement of a person but rather a snapshot in time of their work performance.

But do try to keep the overall tone of your time together upbeat and positive. There is said to be a "positivity ratio" when dealing with human emotion. Some researchers find there needs to be more positive feelings than negative ones by about three to one. This has been widely acclaimed in the mental health field.

That is to say, happy people will experience three times as many positive emotions as negative ones, whereas an equilibrium of emotions may lead to depression. But that number is brought into question or completely discredited by other researchers. After all, how do you measure an emotion?

In terms of interacting with members of a team, that offset number is even higher, about five to one by some researchers. Meaning there need to be five positive statements for every single negative statement if a team is to perform well. I'm not certain I agree with this theory, but I do know the human psyche is fragile and needs a lot of positive reinforcement.

And let's be realistic, this ideal is not always possible. Especially in the fast-paced world of business today where no one has time for five compliments to every one admonition. Suffice it to say, however, it is important to make the mood of the interview as positive as possible.

The goal is not so much that an assessment is written and delivered, but rather guidance is accepted. That means the employee has to be on board with the advice the boss gives. So is it truly necessary to mention **every** deficiency? Do your job, but avoid nitpicking.

When delivering the results of performance, be mindful of what you say and how you say it. Be mindful of saying "I feel you could do better". Feelings are hard to quantify if not impossible. The problem with "constructive criticism" is the only word one hears is, CRITICISM. No one wants to be criticized, so avoid using this term.

Likewise, the word "you" can come across as accusatory so be careful with its use as well. This can be tricky but try to keep the emphasis off of them in your language when a negative is related. Say "Here is what I noticed..." or "Here is how I see it..." Of course, if there are numbers involved, let them speak for themselves.

During the evaluation meeting, provide specific examples of the employee's strengths and areas for improvement. Avoid using vague or general statements and focus on concrete and measurable performance indicators.

To be a legitimate appraisal of work habits, one has to be pragmatic. That means stating the good, the bad and the work to be done. A common process is to deliver negativities in the middle of the conversation and to use positives as bookends at the beginning and end.

With this format, someone is less likely to shut down early. They also leave feeling good about their review. Meanwhile, we hope the critique in the middle will be pondered by the worker. For the most part, I will say this "sandwich" method seems to work out pretty well.

Another discussion format is to commend, recommend and encourage. Begin with all the positives. This helps the staffer to get on board with the observations you have made. Then, instead of calling them negatives, refer to any deficiencies as "growth points" or even some "opportunities." See if there is an agreement between the two of you on these points.

Then, encourage them to correct any growth points. That means creating an action plan or setting goals. Something that can be followed up on later. This could be additional training, shadowing a senior employee for a day or two, or simply committing to better time management. Be certain to encourage them in whatever plan of action you decide.

Some of this alternative language may sound a bit light and fluffy... and it is. But sometimes it's necessary in keeping the lines of communication open.

There is a program that brings me into a women's prison a couple of times a year for some personal development. Tips for job interviews are always a big hit with these soon-to-be-released inmates. The program facilitator often reminds me to be thoughtful with my words as the ladies have been through a lot of trauma and are fragile.

Trauma? Fragile? How about "felon or criminal" I thought. Vulnerability is not what comes to mind when one thinks of prisoners. But to understand the circumstances that got many of them incarcerated and what they have missed since, would make anyone feel as though they were adrift in a sea of negativity.

But no one ever thinks straight if everywhere they look, they see a new threat. When people feel criticized, they either crumble or lash out. And neither is a good option for members of your team.

We don't typically know what life at home is like for an employee. Work may be the most positive place and one may never hear a kind word at home. They may have recently suffered a loss of which you are unaware. So, be thoughtful with your words.

The interview should conclude with a clear action plan that outlines the employee's goals and expectations for the next evaluation period. So, get a sense of their buy-in as to whether they understand what needs to be accomplished. As the boss, you determine the path forward, though the team will be further along that path if there is a certain amount of collaboration. You may be surprised at those who are more critical of themselves than you are.

But a good dialogue can help dispel any misconceptions that might exist. The boss need not always be right all the time, nor should one feel the pressure to be so. If there has been poor communication in the past, it need not be perpetuated in the future.

Having an in-person dialogue allows for an opportunity to dispel any misunderstandings. If an item addressed is in error, fix it. Perhaps it was someone else's fault for not locking the backdoor the night of the robbery, so correct the evaluation.

Many organizations do not consider a follow-up component to the evaluation program. But this is the part where accountability comes into play. An action plan, or for that matter the entire evaluation process is a waste of time without a monitoring of results.

Following up does not necessarily need to be as formal as an interview, though. It can be as simple as asking one how their training went, looking at new production numbers or simply telling them "good job" on the improvements they have made.

I hate to hear about ANNUAL reviews. The third big mistake American businesses make is in the frequency of evaluations. If they are only conducted once a year, I fear too many things are slipping through the cracks.

Yearly may be fine for those who have a lot of seniority or are competent technicians whose job is very routine. The responsibilities of bookkeepers, janitors and security guards probably don't change much from year to year.

Though, it is important to consider how much these employees interact with others. They may be technically proficient but create issues for others when present. In any case, managers should communicate the evaluation frequency and schedule to employees.

Quarterly is preferable. This may sound like a lot, but consider what could happen in just three months. Evaluation periods are not only for workers but also for the boss to take an overall assessment of effectiveness.

Negativity could take root in one staffer and become contagious. Tardiness could become a common practice. Gossip could become widespread. Safety might stop being a priority. Consider evaluations as a good way to keep things running smoothly.

But if quarterly isn't practical, biannually is a good idea. A formal review could be conducted twice a year to identify challenges and work toward solutions. And if a much more casual meeting, say a five-minute sit-down, occurs during those offset quarters, there would be a good plan for keeping things on track.

Those brief, alternate conversations would not necessarily need more paperwork. Just follow up on the guidance given and goals set from three months prior. What progress has been made in the time and how can you help them remain on track?

Of course, a boss should never wait until only the performance reviews to give feedback. They should provide ongoing communication regularly, both positive and constructive, to help employees improve their performance and feel supported.

Recognition throughout the year will do wonders for morale. While corrective actions prevent things from becoming chaotic. So have those vital appraisals as well as that everyday support.

Not every incident calls for a counseling statement or a red flag to be placed in a personnel file. Everyone has bad days or even bad weeks, so if the issues are trivial, they may correct themselves by time of evaluation.

For those instances which may not require correction such as minor dress code infractions or the occasional tardiness, but not a pattern, just make a quick note as to what and when. These notes can serve as a reminder for later on. Think of these employee notes more as a log than a dossier. The intent is to communicate an idea, not to play "gotcha."

But when evaluations are infrequent, both sides will come into it guarded and with walls up. That's not the way to begin any conversation. Whereas having these discussions a few times a year, allows everyone on the team to have a sense of what it is like.

How often were you called into the principal's office in school? More than likely, it was rare but never good. And it's that apprehension we need to avoid.

When someone becomes paranoid as to what a meeting is all about, the imagination can become unhinged. We begin to think the worst, then expect it. That forces us into a defensive position even though we were never offended. Frequency can create a tone of normalcy.

Sometimes evals can also be a bit rushed. This also creates a sense of trepidation. What's happening? Why now? What did I do wrong?

Perhaps management forgot when they were due, HR didn't send a bulletin or maybe the C-suite just has a wild hair. When reviews approach a deadline, or worse are conducted annually, the evaluator may have a lot of items to address.

The subject could misconstrue this as a lack of priority for him or her. In terms of correction, what is intended as advice, might come across as someone being chastised. The lines of true communication are then closed, which makes the review pointless for the employee.

Some in management will detest performance reviews as much as some employees. They state they simply do not have the time to conduct them. In addition to admitting poor time management, what they are truly saying is they do not have a priority to communicate properly with their team.

If it is recommended to change the oil in a car every 5,000 miles, we do so. To not maintain an engine properly, is to ask for greater, more costly issues later. We make the time to do what we must because it is time.

In terms of an exit interview, it can be very resourceful in identifying flaws within the organization. Though it may not be to correct future performance, since the person is leaving the organization, it is still very instrumental yet seldom utilized. But unlike the conversation style of a review, this is truly an interview. So, ask your questions and shut up.

People do not typically leave a company because they are underpaid. After all, they knew what the pay was the day of the interview. This is a common fallacy as to why people quit a job and it can be a costly line of thinking.

Changing jobs is a huge upset for any employee's family. It's like changing cellphone services, selecting a new insurance carrier or going to the dentist. We dread the process. Most employees look for greener pastures because they are undertrained, underutilized or underappreciated.

According to Mercer Human Resource Consulting*, thriving employees are three times more likely to stay with a company that has a strong sense of purpose. In other words, workers want to feel like a part of something more. Something that contributes to society or their personal development. They will be more loyal to a company within which they will grow.

The phenomenon in American business right now is known as the "Great Resignation". But just why are so many leaving current corporations? Granted, some view coming off of the isolation of a worldwide pandemic as a good time to make a transition, if not change careers completely.

But more often than naught, it has something to do with the internal workings of the organization itself. Let's analyze what may occur by taking a look, starting from the top, down.

It may be an issue of low morale or dysfunctional work culture. Each corporation is viewed as a legal entity, a living thing. Being the case, every entity has its distinctive characteristics and personality. The mission statement in the front lobby may say one thing, but the staff will know if it's bullshit.

Top-tier leadership sets the tone for the workplace. As I state in my book, *Managerial Mistakes, Missteps & Misunderstandings*, "Whether morale is good or bad, leadership is responsible". The C suite is the brains of the operation and is ultimately accountable.

Management, whether supervisory or mid-level, may also be at fault. These people are the heart and soul of the enterprise and are in direct contact with employees. But it may not be management itself is toxic, but rather an issue of poor training or the lack of communication skills.

According to Forbes Magazine, the majority of first-time bosses have no business degree or receive NO initial training whatsoever. Those who must report to someone inept, indecisive or lacking empathy, are as frustrated as employees who are in a toxic work environment are fearful.

But, if the workplace is vibrant where respect and good communication are present, it could be the worker himself is simply not a good fit. Perhaps he lacks the skills to complete tasks or simply has a bad attitude.

That being the case, we must look at the hiring practice of the company. Why was this person put in the position in the first place? One has to ask, did HR or the Personnel Department do its job in the first place?

To get a clearer understanding of what went wrong, it is necessary to do an "exit interview". It's just a short conversation with the departing employee to see where the wheels came off. But exit interviews are only effective if three criteria are met. There needs to be an official program, a baseline and a solution for the future.

The first thing to understand about conversations of departure is to DO THEM. And that means all of them or at least the great majority. No employee was ever hired strictly from a questionnaire, so dialogue is a must when one leaves.

Should someone leave on their own, it is a good idea for HR and the boss' boss to sit down, preferably face-to-face, and gain an understanding as to why. Of all the questions to ask, "Why are you leaving" is probably the best. No need to beat around the bush and no need for the entire process to take but just a few minutes.

Of course, if a person is not renewed, fired or otherwise "let go", it may be prudent to conduct a telephone interview a few days later, depending on the circumstances. A good excuse for the call could be administrative, the handling of the final check, insurance, etcetera.

Even a disgruntled former employee might shed light on the overall working conditions. If nothing else, they have an opportunity to vent and are then less likely to badmouth the company. In the age of the Great Resignation, a company's work reputation is vitally important.

But if the employee is simply retiring, it is still worth a conversation. It's a rare opportunity to get the thirty thousand-foot view from someone on the ground for over a decade. After all, they probably don't have to stop working and have nothing to lose by being candid. Few institutions have mandatory retirement these days, so these opinions can be invaluable. That is especially so if they were never known to be disruptive.

This brings us to the second consideration, establishing a baseline. How can management assess why things went from good to bad if it doesn't know whether it was ever good? Annual reviews can serve as benchmarks of productivity, though they should be more frequent than annually.

Most establishments do not conduct these, or if they do it's conducted poorly or even without input from the employee! A sit-down evaluation of work should be conducted with all personnel at least every six months, even if informal.

Finally, corporate leadership and Human Resources should meet quarterly if not monthly to identify and discuss any challenges. Of course, quarterly reports aren't unheard of, but they need to also include an analysis of the well-being of staff. A little forethought and attention can prevent labor disputes and costly turnover later.

But if your people are indeed leaving for more money elsewhere, leadership needs to take note of the competition. As discussed earlier, "If you're not growing, you're dying". Countless businesses have died because they didn't see the warning signs. A good exit interview can be one of those warning signs.

No one said running a team was easy. And I am convinced it takes a special person to even try. Most people are not willing to take the additional responsibility of investing in others while working to achieve organizational goals. Yet, someone has to be the point person for each of these duties.

Common sense can do almost as much good as a management degree. In either case, one has to listen to cohorts, yet avoid every new social fad in business which may derail an organization. With some diligence and a willingness to learn, a manager can achieve success.

About The Author

Corporate trainer, public speaker, and coach Blaine Little has been training for two decades. Founder and CEO of Momentum Seminars Training & Coaching, he has helped thousands of business professionals across the country. He has presented for Schneider Electric, HCA, RE/MAX, Ryman Hospitality (Gaylord Entertainment), Superior Traffic Control, First Community Mortgage, Quik Mart, and dozens of trade associations.

He is a Certified National Trainer, (CNT) as well as a Distinguished Toastmaster (DTM). Blaine is known for keeping training light and fun. After all, that's how people learn. The fact that he is a professional magician doesn't hurt either!

Do you have a large (or small) group that needs to be on the same page with its leadership? *FAST?!?* Momentum Seminars offers corporate training at your facility or the venue of your choosing. Bring the team together in a workshop that promotes the necessary professional skills to make your organization a success and keep it growing well into the 21st century.

LEADERSHIP:

Whether leaders are made or born, one must take an inventory of his or her abilities and assess their greatest resource; the team. Whether you're an inventor with a great idea, a Manager or a Harvard MBA, understand what motivates your people. Take the lead and schedule your training workshop with Momentum Seminars!

- Executive Coaching
- Strategic Planning
- Managerial Training
- First-time Supervisor

TEAM BUILDING:

It takes cohesiveness to move forward. If the members of a team don't work together, the organization will lose. That is perhaps truer in business than so in pro sports. But people need to know WHERE they are going and why. Whether it is remote employees or a project management team that has gotten off track, build the unity and trust every workplace needs.

- Collaboration
- Diversity and Excellence – The IDEA™ Model
- Emotional Intelligence
- Creative Thinking
- Change Management

COMMUNICATION:

Just because you SAID it, doesn't mean they GOT it. Just because you meant it, doesn't mean it's a priority for them. Everyone processes thoughts differently. The chances that the very next person you speak to thinks like YOU are probably slim to none. Learn Meeting Skills and Sales how others think, talk and write so you will be able to better understand them. Be a pro in soliciting feedback in a tactful way that ultimately gets you what you want.

- Sales
- Sales Management
- Customer Service
- Interpersonal
- Meeting Management
- Public Speaking

BUSINESS CONCEPTS:

Momentum Seminars is experienced in training for Sales, Interpersonal Skills, Middle Management, Customer Service and Public Speaking. These core business principles are the lifeblood of any company irrespective of its industry. Yet, Momentum will CUSTOMIZE a workshop session specifically for what your organization needs. Invest in your people by bringing us into your organization today!

Be certain to get a copy of Blaine's managerial book,
Avoiding Managerial Mistakes, Missteps &
Misunderstandings;
The Essential Guide for All Managers

*Footnotes and Citations

Harter, Jim. "Employee Engagement vs. Employee Satisfaction and Organizational Culture." *Gallup.com*, Gallup, 24 Mar. 2023, https://www.gallup.com/workplace/236366/right-culture-not-employee-satisfaction.aspx.

Carnegie, Dale, 1888-1955. How to Win Friends and Influence People. New York :Simon & Schuster, 2009.

Fry, Richard. "Millennials Are the Largest Generation in the U.S. Labor Force." *Pew Research Center*, Pew Research Center, 27 July 2020, https://www.pewresearch.org/fact-tank/2018/04/11/millennials-largest-generation-us-labor-force/.

Team, Fear. "Government Corruption, Fear for Loved Ones, Civil Unrest Top Fears in America - a Majority of Americans Believe Places Can Be Haunted by Spirits ." *The Voice of Wilkinson*, 14 Oct. 2021, https://blogs.chapman.edu/wilkinson/2021/10/14/government-corruption-fear-for-loved-ones-civil-unrest-top/.

Nordstrom, David Sturt and Todd. "10 Shocking Workplace Stats You Need to Know." *Forbes*, Forbes Magazine, 12 Oct. 2022, https://www.forbes.com/sites/davidsturt/2018/03/08/10-shocking-workplace-stats-you-need-to-know/.

Eustachewich, Lia. "Coca-Cola Slammed for Diversity Training That Urged Workers to Be 'Less White'." *New York Post*, New York Post, 23 Feb. 2021, https://nypost.com/2021/02/23/coca-cola-diversity-training-urged-workers-to-be-less-white/.

DeSimone, John Pitonyak and Rob. "How to Engage Frontline Managers." *Gallup.com*, Gallup, 10 Mar. 2023, https://www.gallup.com/workplace/395210/engage-frontline-managers.aspx.

Christopher F. Rufo is a senior fellow at the Manhattan Institute and a contributing editor of City Journal. Sign up for his newsletter here. "Raytheon Adopts Critical Race Theory." *City Journal*, 6 July 2021, https://www.city-journal.org/raytheon-adopts-critical-race-theory.

Sandberg, Sheryl, and Nell Scovell. *Lean in: Women, Work, and the Will to Lead.* First edition. New York: Alfred A. Knopf, 2013.

"Why Workplace Purpose Matters for Your Business." *Mercer*, https://www.mercer.us/our-thinking/healthcare/why-workplace-purpose-matters-for-your-business.html.

Edited by Lois Little

Made in the USA
Columbia, SC
29 October 2024

44982816R00115